TESLA'S OPERA
The real, stranger-than-fiction Nikola Tesla

Edited by Mir Seidel

Fomite Press
Burlington, VT 2025

ISBN-13: 978-1-967022-09-0
Library of Congress Control Number: 2025942361

Fomite Press
58 Peru Street
Burlington, VT 05401
09-03-2025

CONTENTS

An opera about Nikola Tesla 1

Prologue: Dante Lasciato Fuori
    un Moderno, Andrei Codrescu 3

Jon Gibson, *Violet Fire*'s Composer 5

Tesla: The Libretto, Mir Seidel 11

Directing *Violet Fire*, Terry O'Reilly 27

Violet Fire, A Dance Critic's View, Merilyn Jackson 38

Conducting Nikola Tesla's opera,
    Ana Zorana Brajović 45

Violet Fire, the Libretto 47

Scene Summaries and Notes 50

Scene 1   53

Scene 2   57

Scene 3   63

Scene 4   71

Scene 5   83

Scene 6   93

Appendices   97

Appendix 1: Nikola Tesla: A Biographical Timeline 99

Appendix 2: Tesla and Gernsback: An Untold Story
    of the Birth of Modern Science Fiction 101

Appendix 3: *Violet Fire* Collaborators and Performers . . . 109

Appendix 4: Resources 115

Acknowledgments 117

AN OPERA ABOUT NIKOLA TESLA

Tesla's Opera

DANTE LASCIATO FUORI UN MODERNO

Andrei Codrescu

There is redhot iron chair in the Lake of Fire
in the Heart & Idea Thieves section of Dante's Hell
reserved for Elon Musk in punishment for the veil
of linguistic rubber and gauze he laid
in automobile form over the memory of the great
Nikola Tesla the Serbian genius who immigrated
to America to enact the splendors of electricity
and other world-changing flights of divine insight
whispered to him by angels soon flagged by the FBI.
What's in the name you say? Everything. I will
now reveal what the ghost of Tesla whispered in my ear:
"All these one-syllable men are bad aliens sent
to earth to harvest us, especially Gates, Bush and Musk!
They were so named to be easy to remember. These bad
aliens unlike the beneficent spirits who spoke to me,

are here to replace our languages with one-syllable grunts

and then just numbers." Since then I turn over the name

of every shiny new thing to see what human greatness

it has buried. Among them, most grievous of them all

is the great Tesla overlaid into oblivion by the Musk car.

Inspired by the brilliant Miriam who in her turn was awed

by the real Tesla we will lift that vile motor off our genius

and raise Musk himself into the red-hot iron chair in the Lake of Fire

where roasted for his onomastic sins he'll spend eternity!"

Andrei Codrescu is a novelist, essayist, poet and filmmaker. He has published four novels, one of which, Messiah, *includes Nikola Tesla as a character, three book-length essays, and numerous books of poetry, stories, and essays. He was a longtime senior commentator for NPR's* All Things Considered *and won a Peabody Award for his film* Road Scholar. *His latest book,* How to Live Under Fascism: New Poems & Photographs, *is out from Black Widow Press.*

JON GIBSON, *VIOLET FIRE*'S COMPOSER

Mir Seidel

The music of Jon Gibson (1940-2020) is characterized by seeming contradictions: spareness and transparency along with eloquent harmonic textures; reserve along with deeply expressive emotion. In creating the score for *Violet Fire*, the opera about Nikola Tesla, he brought these qualities into an exquisite balance, evoking the elegance and power of Tesla's inventions, the vastness of his imagination, and the human emotions of an inventor who held himself largely aloof from them. In working on the score, Jon intended to create an accessible piece that could appeal to people on many levels of musical interest.

Here's the statement he wrote about the opera:

> The music to *Violet Fire* should sound familiar to most listeners, as it uses harmonies and rhythms that can be found in classical, jazz and popular western music, and is performed by traditional music forces—voice and instruments, along with some sampled and treated sounds. The music can be described as pulsing sonic fields over which the libretto is sung. Texture, repetition, stasis, rhythm and melody establish themselves and then change, sometimes gradually, sometimes abruptly in an ongoing,shifting series of musical elements.

His work revealed his own personal integration of the minimalist experimentation

he was part of. Jon was a founding member of the Philip Glass Ensemble, playing with them from 1968 on. That year, Philip Glass wrote the saxophone solo *Gradus* for him. A gifted multi-instrumentalist, he performed early works (many written for him) by other minimalist pioneers including Steve Reich, Terry Riley, and La Monte Young.

He was a consummate collaborator. Jon performed and/or collaborated with such composer/performers as Christian Wolff, Frederick Rzewski, Garret List, David Behrman, Petr Kotik, Thomas Buckner, "Blue" Gene Tyranny, Harold Budd, Alvin Curran, Arthur Russell, Peter Zummo, Barbara Benary, and Jaron Lanier. He worked with director JoAnne Akalaitas as composer on the music-theater piece, *Voyage of the Beagle*.

Jon had a gift for creating soundscapes that responded seamlessly to the other elements—and a particular affinity for creating music for dance. He wrote scores and performed with numerous dancer/choreographers, including Marilyn Wood (*Seagram Building Event*, 1972), Nancy Topf (*The Great Outdoors*, 1976), Margaret Jenkins (*Equal Time*, 1976), Merce Cunningham (*Fractions*, 1977, and various "Events"), Lucinda Childs (*Relative Calm*, 1981), Elaine Summers (*Solitary*

Geometry, 1983), Simone Forti (*Framing Music*, 1992), Elisabetta Vittoni (*La Spezia*, 1993) and Nina Winthrop on several works in addition to *Violet Fire (Stalling Into Elation, Prism, Three Lives and Something, Exissensuelle*, and others.

His recordings include *Jon Gibson: In Good Company*, Point Music; *Jon Gibson: Two Solo Pieces + Melody III & IV + Song 1*, New Tone; *Virtuosity With Purpose*, S.E.M. Ensemble, Ear-Rational; *A Confederacy of Dances Vol. 2*, Einstein Records; *New Music New York 1979*, Orange Mountain Music; and *Criss X Cross*, Tzadic Records, among others. He also collaborated or performed on recordings with Steve Reich, Philip Glass, Frederick Rzweski, Garret List, Harold Budd, David Behrman, Alvin Curran, Barbara Benary, Rande-Raine Reusche, Peter Zummo, Robert Ashley, Arthur Russell, Annea Lockwood, and New Music Ensemble.

Some years after the productions in Belgrade and New York, Jon oversaw a studio recording of *Violet Fire*, performed by some of the original principal singers including Scott Murphree, who played Nikola Tesla, and Peter Stewart, who sang Mark Twain's part. The recording is available from Orange Mountain Music. Mick Rossi, a composer, conductor and longtime member of the Philip Glass Ensemble, worked with him as a producer and conductor on the recording. He offers this remembrance of Jon Gibson:

> I have had the privilege of sharing stages around the world with my friend and colleague Jon Gibson as a fellow member of the Philip Glass Ensemble for almost twenty-five years. I can say that his music, and subsequently *Violet Fire*, is very much like him and his artwork: concise, transparent, self-effacing and shy. He, along with his contemporaries La Monte Young, Terry Riley, Laurie Anderson, Steve Reich, and Philip Glass, introduced a complex, adventurous language to the New York loft scene and beyond. And, unsurprisingly, Jon and I spent many a time (and several margaritas!) discussing the plan at Lupe's in SoHo for finally getting *Violet Fire* recorded after the BAM run. Jon has left a quiet legacy. He was definitely a one-off and is dearly missed.

Terry O'Reilly, *Violet Fire*'s director, knew and worked with Jon Gibson for many years. Here is his reminiscence of Jon and his place in the experimental environment of California and New York that shaped him:

Jon Gibson's music was largely composed when I came in to direct *Violet Fire* for the Temple University showcase in 2004, but we had worked together as far back as 1977 in a dance performance at St. Mark's Church In-the-Bowery.

As a part of the southern wave of artists coming to New York City around 1970, I can say that music was a major part of the allure. Philip Glass, who had trained with Ravi Shankar in Paris, was a big fan of Clifton Chenier and Zydeco music, and two of the founding members of the Philip Glass Ensemble, composers Richard Peck and Richard (Dickie) Landry, were up from the Mississippi Delta and Louisiana coast.

Jon, also a founding member, was already a key member of the hugely influential San Francisco Tape Music Center. Jon was an original performer for Terry Riley's *In C* along with Steve Reich, Pauline Oliveros, Stuart Dempster, Morton Subotnick and others. These composers wrote for and were inspired by one another. Jon was the first Western musician to train himself in circular breathing for the flute and saxophone. The long notes that Philip could play on the keyboard were at once then possible for Jon to play, and broadened the possible for what the music could be. Jon could play notes that other musicians could only imagine.

All of his early albums were recorded on Chatham Square Records, an independent label established by Philip and others working with technical collaborator Kurt Munkacsi. Kurt fine-tuned the sound for Mabou Mines, where I was part of the company, and was also a go-to sound engineer for John Lennon, the Fluxus musicians, and performers including La Monte Young and Steve Reich, Robert Rauschenberg, Merce Cunningham, John Cage and a whole host of visual artists crossing borders.

I remember Jon playing for me a recording of *In C* that was made in Shanghai, China in 1989, entirely performed with Chinese instrumentation. Jon delighted in its force, life and energy. This performance of a piece born in San Francisco and out of that time and place, had been recorded months before Tiananmen Square, and went on to be passed around on cassettes for years as an underground phenomenon.

Much as a playwright will write for and be inspired by a particular actor, the same can be said for composers and musicians. As it is in jazz, theater and dance performance, the spirit is: "I feed you, you feed me." There was a thin and very porous membrane between the artists of Jon's generation working in Anna Halprin's Dancers' Workshop, the Actors Workshop, the San Francisco Mime Troupe and the Tape Music Center. Everyone was gladly in each other's business. A significant part of that San Francisco scene was reconstituted in 1970 in New York City. Philip Glass, a founding member of Mabou Mines, put together his ensemble in 1970 with Richard Peck, Dickie Landry, Jon Gibson, Joan La Barbara, Michael Riesman and others.

I remember Philip doing pickup work as a plumber and putting in marathon hours driving a cab to ensure that the salaries of the members of the group were paid, while Dickie, between gigs, was a sometime Cajun cook at Food Restaurant in Soho, and Richard Peck and I were dishwashers there. Richard made music with the cutlery. Fellow Mabou Miners Suzanne Harris, Barbara Dilley, Cynthia Hedstrom, Ruth Maleczech, and Joanne Akalaitis were all cooks along with Gordon. Food Restaurant was the brainchild of Gordon Matta-Clark, Tina Girouard and Carol Goodden, conceived as a way for artists to support and feed one another. This was Jon Gibson's world. It was a hub for the Fluxus Movement, a big frame and alliance for all manner of visual and performing artists. I feed you, you feed me. The spirit of all this was that we were setting about to create the world we wanted to live in.

To give you an idea of his work, for his performances at Saint Marks Church/Dancespace in 1977, Jon literally played the church. Positioned in the balcony, drumsticks in hand, he played the wooden railings, the pillars, a chair he liked, even the body of abandoned church organ. It was for him as if the 180-year-old church were a xylophone of notes and echoes waiting to be played. I can remember him stepping around in the balcony before and during rehearsals, tapping, listening, returning, testing the sound of things, finding the notes in anything wooden, whatever was metal, the ringing of an acetylene bottle, this and not too much. The challenge was to not pick up his alto sax or his flute—although during performance, he indeed played his instruments in a few sections.

Terry's memory of Jon "playing" the church itself makes me remember how I thought of him composing the music for *Violet Fire*, working from my libretto: listening deeply, finding the sound hidden in each word or phrase, pulling those sounds into a coherent, surprising yet elegant whole.

Those of us who worked on *Violet Fire* with Jon Gibson miss him dearly, and are so grateful for his indelible contribution to the opera.

TESLA: THE LIBRETTO

Mir Seidel

When I first heard about Nikola Tesla, back in the twentieth century, I was surprised. How was it that this man—whose stream of inventions and ideas laid the foundation for our electrified lives—wasn't universally known, as Thomas Edison was? How could it be that the man who discovered the means for generating and transmitting alternating current, who held basic patents in other fields including radio, robotics, and even computer circuitry, wasn't a household name?

Not only that, but Tesla's outsized personality and life made him a tantalizing figure. Born into a modest Serbian family in Croatia, he rode a series of groundbreaking scientific breakthroughs to become world-famous around the turn of the last century. Featured in the scientific and popular press, he moved in the highest levels of New York society before his fortunes shrank. Though he had friends, he never married or fell in love—except, by his own account, with a particular white pigeon.

Only an opera, I thought, could capture the extremes and the surreal quality of Tesla's life and imagination. Naïvely, I thought a project like this could help bring Tesla's story to a wider audience and restore his fame. And I'd seen enough new opera and music theater, through Philadelphia's American Music Theater Festival, to sense what was possible. I knew I couldn't write the music, so I started by writing a libretto.

Nikola Tesla reading, seated in front of the spiral coil of a high-frequency transformer at his Houston Street Laboratory in New York, 1896

In a stroke of luck, I discovered the work of the composer Jon Gibson, whose music for singers and dancers had an expansive, dreamy quality that seemed just right for Tesla. I was thrilled when he agreed to work on the opera. We gradually added collaborators, including director Terry O'Reilly, who helped put together the first performance in Philadelphia, in 2004, at Temple University in a combined collaboration of faculty, students, and the Relâche instrumental ensemble there.

Thanks to Terry's groundwork and vision, the opera *Violet Fire* moved forward to a full professional premiere in Belgrade, as part of the city's celebration of Tesla's 150th birthday in 2006. There I learned firsthand how Tesla is revered as a national hero in both Serbia and Croatia. A few months later, the opera returned for a full US premiere featuring the singers from Serbia, costumes and sets by Boris Čakširan, and conducted by Ana Zorana Brajović. The opera played to full audiences in all locations, and received good coverage in the press—although I'm not sure it made a significant difference in Tesla's public profile.

Now, nearly twenty years later, we find ourselves in a different world. Tesla has become a household word spoken around the world thanks to Tesla Motors, the electric vehicle company named after him. But the appropriation of his name,

Projection image for Violet Fire: *Patent diagram in negative view for Electric Magnetic Motor, No. 382,279, Patented by Nikola Tesla, May 1, 1888*

no doubt originally meant as an homage to a pioneer in electricity, has curdled thanks to the company's connection to its megalomaniacal owner.

The trajectory of the electric car company, yoked to its owner, has put a stain on Tesla the man, and obscured the compelling story we wanted to put forward with the opera. At best, some people now think Tesla is the inventor of the electric car, which he isn't. At worst, not only are his actual contributions still in shadow—his more intangible qualities are too. Tesla's grand visions were matched by an equal generosity of spirit, not the greed and desire for power that drives the head of Tesla Motors. Tesla consistently put his considerable income into new work, a factor in his poverty in later life. He aimed to improve people's lives in numerous ways, especially through his unrealized dream of providing free energy around the globe. Even his proposed machines of war were meant as a deterrent to promote peace.

We need *that* Tesla.

We hope that in revisiting *Violet Fire*, this book will inspire readers with a deeper view of Tesla, one that integrates his world-changing achievements with his mystical side—the man who saw visions of flames as a child, who worked out

13

his inventions in his mind's eye, and who was hailed as a "Prince of the Violet Fire" by the spiritualist author Margaret Storm.

The White Dove

Tesla moved to the United States in 1884 and settled in New York City. His most influential discoveries were behind him by the 1920s. In his later years, supported by a stipend from the Yugoslavian government, he could often be found feeding pigeons in different parks in Manhattan. He kept cages in his hotel room, where he nursed sick birds back to health.

It was learning about Tesla's friendship with a certain white pigeon that brought home to me the stranger-than-fiction quality of his story. The bird would find him wherever he went in the city's parks. He confided to a reporter, "I loved her as a man loved a woman, and she loved me"—an instance of intimacy he'd felt toward animals since his childhood, growing up on his family's farm.

One night, his beloved pigeon flew to his window and settled on the ledge. He knew, he told the reporter, that she was going to die. Before that happened, the inventor saw an intense, dazzling light emanating from her eyes, "a light more intense than I had ever produced in my laboratory."

Projection image from Violet Fire, *Scene 4: Tesla's pigeon and light bulb superimposed on illuminated skyline*

This story offered a seeming paradox—a scientist, whose work has affected the entire world, who was subject to visions that might have visited medieval saints. Only an opera, I thought, with its grand scale and over-the-top passions, could encompass a full sense of this complex, remarkable man.

Later, after I'd revised the libretto several times, the pigeon nudged me to another insight that would shape the opera: I had to let the bird sing. She would appear at times through the story, reminding Tesla of the element of wonder and intuitive connection with nature that fueled his work. This would offer a counterweight to the grand scale of some of his technological projects and proposals.

Some of the Dove's lines are adapted from Tesla's observations of sky and weather in his *Colorado Springs Notes*, the journal he kept during his year of research into high-frequency electrical generation and transmission at that isolated location, known for its prodigious natural lightning.

Tesla's relationship with the white pigeon also shaped the structure of the libretto. It would be framed as a series of memories that come to him while he sits on a bench in the park, surrounded by pigeons. Scene 1 would be a kind of prologue, with Tesla grieving the destruction of his tower at Wardenclyffe, on the tip of Long Island, in 1918. The Wardenclyffe project was meant to be a proof of concept for what would be a worldwide system of free information and energy transfer—a foreshadowing of our globally Internet-connected world. The loss of Tesla's tower marks the transition to his later life, with his great achievements behind him.

The next scene would place him in the park, remembering his earliest breakthroughs. Then we would revisit some of the people he knew, including his socialite friend Katharine Johnson and Mark Twain, who recognized the grand and strange potentials in Tesla's work. Later scenes would include the author Margaret Storm, the death of the pigeon he loved, and his own farewell to life. At the end, he is invited to relinquish the desire to actualize his visions, allowing some of his ideas to return to "the dream-bank" of our collective imagination.

Tesla's Wardenclyffe Tower with operating station designed by Stanford White, 1904.

Tesla on the bench (Scene 2)

In Scene 2, Tesla sits brooding on a park bench, with a view of Bryant Park projected behind him. The Reporter sketches Tesla's situation, his words adapted from actual headlines and news stories about Tesla, describing great achievements and great disappointments. The White Dove appears to Tesla and they sing together, their words suggesting communion within waves of electromagnetic energy. Their musical duet floats on long, plangent harmonic lines that trace a combination of yearning and elation in that moment.

Here and throughout the opera, a stream of video images accompanied the action. At different times they might embody Tesla's cascade of ideas and visions, pointing to their more virtual, potential state of being; offer homage to his intensely visual imagination; suggest a dream-world existing alongside our everyday world; and at times, fill out the setting and exposition.

All this was brought into powerful form by video artists Sarah Drury and Jen Simmons, who joined the project in its first production at Temple. They created a dynamic, visually dense video "score" that runs through the opera's entire eighty minutes and six scenes. In the performances, I felt an amazing synergy between the music and sound design, the singers, costumes and sets,

Projection image from Violet Fire, *Scene 4: Illustration of Nikola Tesla surrounded by rays of light, from* New York World, *1894, in wooden frame, against field of stars*

and video, weaving a holistic sense of Tesla and his story. Stills from the video projections shown in this book, along with images showing their interaction with the performers, will suggest some of that wonderful unity.

One of Terry O'Reilly's directorial insights was to have the Dove portrayed by two performers—sometimes at the same time. A singer dressed in white, appearing on a raised platform, would sing, while a white-clad dancer would embody the pigeon's movements. This doubling, derived from Noh theater, put the Dove in an otherworldly space, oscillating between earth and sky, the physical and the spiritual.

In the opera, Tesla's first encounter with the Dove leads him to the memory of his first great breakthrough, envisioning a generator capable of producing alternating current. This had come to him in 1881, when Tesla was in Budapest working at his first job.

He'd been aware of the unsatisfactory performance of direct-current generators, which limited any wider adoption. He sensed the answer lay in using alternating current, something no one had tried yet. Obsessed with this problem, he worked until he suffered a breakdown that involved strange symptoms, including

Performance photo from Violet Fire, *Scene 2, showing two White Doves (dancer Joanna Kotze and soprano Mirjana Jovanović Stojanović), National Theater, Belgrade, July 2006. Photo by Srdjan Mihič*

abnormal sensitivities to the smallest sounds, vibrations, and objects around him, along with a wildly fluctuating pulse.

While walking in a city park, he stopped to watch the sunset with a friend and began to recite a verse from Goethe's *Faust*. At that moment, he froze, finally seeing the answer to the question that had made him so sick. It was a vision of Tesla's uniquely elegant solution: a series of alternating pulses that pushed each other around an axle in a frictionless motion.

This, combined with his later invention of the electrical transformer, would make possible the generation and distribution of electrical energy that we still use today. In the opera's video, evolving images of diagrams seen against the sky make his inspiration visible. Tesla and the Dove celebrate the moment, with the chorus joining in, all singing the verse from Goethe together. The music changes here, shifting into buoyant song.

My dear and silent friend (Scene 3)

Tesla moved to New York in 1884 with hopes of bringing his invention to the world. Others have chronicled how he went to work for Thomas Edison, but then

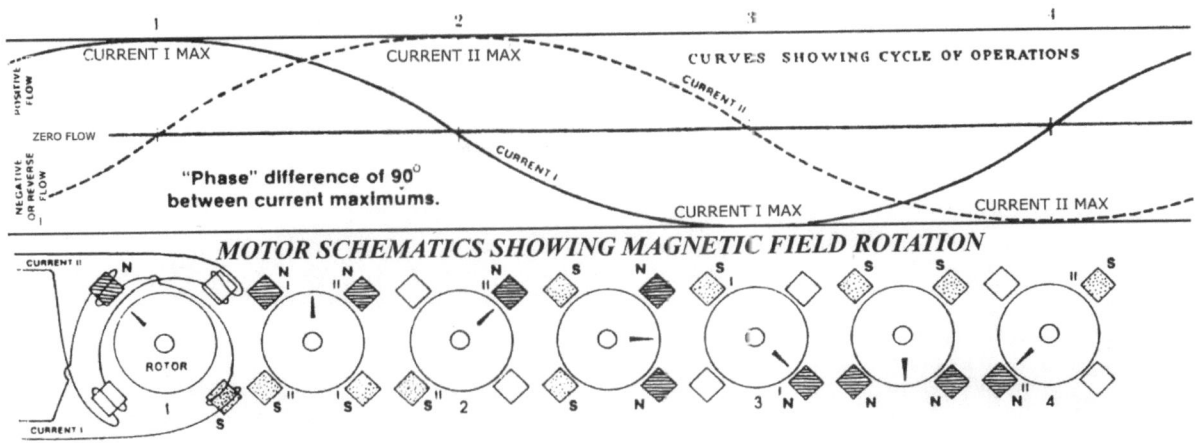

Diagram showing rotating magnetic field inside Tesla's alternating current motor

fell out with him and went out on his own. I decided not to involve Edison, who has already received so much attention. After several years of struggling, Tesla received a tidal wave of recognition for his alternating-current generator, and was celebrated for his stunning electrical demonstrations, capturing the public's imagination with promises of unimagined technological progress.

He became a celebrity, moving through New York society. Robert Johnson, editor of *Century* magazine, embraced Tesla as a friend and wrote about him and his work in the magazine. His wife Katharine invited Tesla to dinner and other events, including the opera. Although she attempted to fix him up with various young debutantes, her letters to him reveal that she herself cared deeply about the dashing and charismatic inventor.

In Scene 3, Katharine Johnson addresses Tesla in her own words. Her own melancholy, and her desire for connection with her "dear and silent friend" who too often would disappear into his work, speaks to Tesla's human isolation. (He attributed his avoidance of marriage or any serious relationships to a fear of compromising his intense focus on his work.)

The distance between Katharine and Tesla also stands in for what I saw as a revealing back-story to another of Tesla's major breakthroughs—his invention

Performance photo from Violet Fire, *Scene 3, showing Katharine Johnson (Dragana Stanković), National Theater, Belgrade, July 2006. Photo by Srdjan Mihič*

of radio. (His foundational patents predated Marconi's by several years.) As with the alternating-current generator, in the 1890s Tesla became obsessed with the possibility of wireless transmission of electrical signals. Again, his relentless work affected his health. After months of overwork he fell into a heavy sleep, and found when he woke up that he could remember nothing of his life after his earliest memories.

Over time, he was able to recover later and later memories, always focusing on his mother. Tesla had been close to his mother, from whom he'd inherited his curiosity and interest in building things, and during that time of intense work he had received word that her health was failing. He accepted invitations to lecture in London and Paris, then traveled across Europe and was able to spend a few hours with his mother. Early the next morning he experienced a vision of his mother's death and heavenly ascension, which coincided with her moment of death.

Soon after that, Tesla gave a lecture outlining the principles of radio broadcasting. The coincidence of the inventor's yearning for connection to his faraway, dying mother and his work on a method of communicating across great distances struck me as both hugely poignant and meaningful. At this point in the opera, Tesla calls out to his mother, seeming to mistake Katharine for her; at the scene's end, he finally answers Katharine's request for "a word from you" with a one-word answer: "Broadcast."

One hundred thousand volts (Scene 4)

This scene shows Tesla at the height of his fame, appearing as a kind of electrical wizard. With the inventor surrounded by a chorus of breathless onlookers, Mark Twain offers him praise in words partly taken from his *Letters from the Earth*. That work is actually a searingly bitter satire on humanity as seen from the perspective of God—one reason Twain didn't publish it in his lifetime.

But part of its opening passage, which starts, "He lifted his hand and from it burst a fountain-spray of fire," seemed to me like a great, over-the-top take on Tesla's seemingly supernatural powers. The music matches this triumphal form, with Twain and Tesla proclaiming the inventor's accomplishments and the chorus crying out on cue.

In fact, the two men were friends and mutual admirers. Twain had visited Tesla's laboratory around the time of his announcement of the principles of radio. The author quickly grasped the revolutionary promise of the inventor's work and a few years later, even offered to license some of Tesla's inventions in Europe.

In this scene Tesla stands on a raised platform, turning dials, and a stream of video images suggest the raw power of the energy he was working with. Twain's paean to Tesla celebrates his ability to extend human dominion over nature, extending into its hidden aspects. This identifies the inventor squarely within the modern bias toward technological progress, even extending to using devices for destructive ends. Both Twain and Tesla did speak about using his some of his inventions (unbuilt) to act as weapons to end war. His singing "I can split the earth like an apple" echoes his belief that his experiments with resonance could lead to ever-expanding vibrations which could have literally world-shaking effects.

Performance photo from Violet Fire, *Scene 4, l-r: Mark Twain (Miodrag Jovanović), Reporter (Nenad Nenić), Katharine Johnson (Dragana Stanković), and Tesla (Scott Murphree), National Theater, Belgrade, July 2006. Photo by Srdjan Mihič*

In contrast to this, Margaret Storm—who wrote the 1959 book *The Return of the Dove*—enters here to offer her own version of Tesla's superhuman attributes. Storm wrote that Tesla was born on Venus and spirited to Earth in a flying saucer as an infant. She hailed him as "Prince of the Violet Fire," identifying him with the highest-frequency color on the electromagnetic spectrum, as well as with the violet/indigo color of the highest chakra in yogic tradition. Writers including Robert Anton Wilson and others have explored this mystical side of Tesla, and others talk about his "secret" work on time travel, antigravity, and other fringe-science subjects.

Storm sings and moves to a seductive tango, wooing Tesla and the audience with Gibson's sinuous vocal lines. But her mythologizing words are no more successful in capturing his attention than the longing thoughts of Katharine Johnson. Margaret Storm's formulations can sound silly, but to me they also offer a wonderfully poetic way to approach this side of Tesla, and his lifelong attraction to exploring ever-higher frequencies.

The world was not prepared (Scene 5)

The next scene returns to Tesla in the park with his pigeons. Now, instead of traveling through memories, we are with him at this moment, past his time of great achievements. Tesla had always been able to raise money from investors for his projects—J. P. Morgan backed his Wardenclyffe project, for example. But he spent most of it on his work, and continued to live in luxurious style even after the investors disappeared. Hearing of his financial difficulties, George Westinghouse arranged to pay him a consulting stipend, which along with a pension from the Yugoslavian government supported Tesla until his death in 1943.

Reporters continued to seek him out, and Tesla slipped into the role of a futurist, making sweeping predictions on technology and society. The Reporter sings some of the headlines describing those predictions, involving communication with Mars, sending power at a distance, and his "Death Ray for Defense." Katharine Johnson voices concerns about the danger of his harnessing electromagnetism, with unknown and possible injurious effects. Tesla, who in life never expressed such concerns, defends his work, insisting it would bring "peace for all—an end to suffering." While Margaret Storm continues her siren song of adulation, the Dove joins in with Katharine, singing about an "Earth out of tune."

The death of Tesla's pigeon here, a painful moment beautifully embodied in Nina Winthrop's choreography, aligns with these darker implications of Tesla's work.

The lightning is still there (Scene 6)

In the final scene, Tesla has moved beyond regret and loss, and begins by reaching back in time for a childhood memory. Tesla had shared this memory with Pola Fotic, the young daughter of the Yugoslav ambassador, in a letter written in 1939, a few years before his death. In it he described his first experience of electricity, astonished by a shower of sparks off the

Performance photo from Violet Fire, *Scene 4: Tesla (Scott Murphree) standing against field of stars, National Theater, Belgrade, July 2006. Photo by Srdjan Mihič*

fur of the family cat. "Is Nature a giant cat?" he recalled wondering. "If so, who strokes its back?" It's a kind of valedictory to his life's work, returning to its first spark nearly eighty years earlier.

The principal singers and chorus gather around Tesla as the Dove beckons him to join her on the higher planes. They call out his triumphs and his unrealized ideas, inviting him to "lay down the fire," the blinding light that has attracted him all his life, to finally let go.

Sink into the dream-bank

Tesla's legacy, I believe, has a dual quality. There is the one we live with, almost so ubiquitous that we don't notice it any more. We exist in an alternating-current world, set to a background frequency of 50-60 Hertz, based on Tesla's research into the frequency of the ionosphere. Our remote controls are built on Tesla's first patents. Radio stations send out messages at a distance, as he determined they could.

Projection image from Violet Fire, *Scene 6: Church near Tesla's birthplace, Smiljan, now Croatia, superimposed on image of land nearby*

At the same time, he threw out a stream of ideas that were never realized, some never tested. These were as large, or sometimes larger in their projected scope than those that were built. There's his spine-tingling idea of drawing electrical energy down directly from the upper atmosphere, not to mention the particle-beam weapon he claimed would end war with its defensive capabilities. His Wardenclyffe tower pointed toward a never-achieved global network for sharing of free streams of data and energy—anticipating the Internet, yet eerily different from it.

What happened to that aspect of his legacy? There are clues that, to me, point in a tantalizing direction. After *Violet Fire*'s production, I pursued these threads, which suggest that Tesla's sprawling imagination fed the development of the modern genre of science fiction. The connecting link is Hugo Gernsback, the publisher (and minor inventor himself) who grasped the scope and elegance of Tesla's mainly wireless approach. It was Gernsback who commissioned Tesla to write his autobiography and published it in serial form in his magazine, the *Electrical Experimenter*, and who printed Tesla's articles and predictions. In the 1920s,

Gernsback launched *Amazing Stories*, acknowledged as the first science fiction magazine. (The science fiction genre's Hugo Awards are named after him.)

The article I wrote about this unsung Tesla-Gernsback connection, which appeared in the *New York Review of Science Fiction*, is reprinted in the Appendix. I see Tesla as a kind of godfather to modern science fiction, a field that's become a cultural proving ground for our imaginal stance toward the future.

This doesn't wrap up the mystery of Tesla, though. To me, Tesla was a kind of shaman of electromagnetism, who existed in a mental liminal space where the possible and the improbable coexisted easily and without prejudice. The question of which of his inventions and ideas would be widely adopted is a different one, pulling in other actors. George Westinghouse, for example, understood the potential of Tesla's AC motor and was responsible for its successful scaling-up into national and international use.

In another sense, we are part of Tesla's chorus, marveling at his visions, entering his dream, and in some way making collective choices as to which parts will be realized in our shared world, and which will remain in the world's dream-bank—perhaps to reemerge sometime in the future.

This Tesla, both scientist and shaman, is the one we need to remember and appreciate.

Mir Seidel wrote the librettos for Violet Fire *and for the opera* Judgment of Midas. *She has also published a novel and short stories. See more under Collaborators in the Appendix.*

DIRECTING *VIOLET FIRE*

Terry O'Reilly

Nikola Tesla, visionary icon

When I arrived in Belgrade to work on rehearsals for Violet Fire, I found the face of the hero of the opera I had come to make—pictured on the money. Yes, there was Nikola Tesla on the 100-dinar note, along with his AC motor and his white pigeon. Imagine that. Born 150 years before, to a Serbian family in what is now Croatia, before even the birth of the state of Yugoslavia—here Nikola, who became a US citizen, was pictured on the face of Serbian money. And everyone in that city had stories of him. A cab driver told me, once I let him know what we were working on at his city's National Theater, that Tesla loved opera. That he had visions of the sun, and turning circuits, and heard the voice of angels. (These would be Mezzo-soprano angels.)

This driver told me that Tesla had wired the auditorium with a new invention of his, the microphone, and brought the cables to the square outside the opera house and connected them to another invention of his, the loudspeaker. In this way people who could never afford to attend could hear grand opera, for free. His stories both reflected and embellished the truth, as long-told family stories do. Tesla scholars told me of a whole range of medical devices employing electricity in the archives, tested but that had been never been brought into use. Again and again, we see the generosity of his spirit and his desire to make the fruits of his inventions available to all. How much larger than life can a person be?

At times it seemed that everyone in the country had their stories; it was like walking into a da Vinci notebook in the oral tradition. Artists in the Americas also revered him. Marina Abramović, the Serbian-born conceptual artist, wanted to know what the opera would look like; her brother was the former director of the Tesla Museum in Belgrade, which gave us entrée to the images of the archives, and important to me, a stamp of cultural approval. Marina had created a tribute performance for Tesla at the Museum and donated the proceeds to preservation work for the archives.

Artists loved Tesla because he was a quite literally, a visionary—a quality shared by all scientists but rarely in such abundance. Working on Jon and Miriam's opera with choreographer Nina Winthrop and Serbian conductor Ana Zorana Brajović, I began to think and speak of him as a poet of science. His originality, and his gift for showmanship, gave his work a mythic dimension. Carter Burwell, composer for the Coen Brothers films and many others, told me of one of Tesla's "performances" in his West Broadway laboratory in New York City: he set up a vibration engine that so shook the building, people feared it would crack and fall apart and pandemonium ensued. Tesla with a flourish stopped his engine and quiet returned.

He was a scientist who went out on his own to raise money, very like his friend Mark Twain who started his own publishing house and then went on, for the first time, something called a book tour to sell his product. Twain dressed always in white, always recognizable, and Tesla, spectacularly tall in formal evening clothes, looked very like the magician that in many ways he was. Cartoonists of the era capped him, with another first, the mad scientist.

In a studio performance at Mabou Mines, where I am artistic director, Carter Burwell also conceived, directed, and composed a piece about Tesla, and his very modern wrangle with Thomas Edison over the assertion that alternating current was superior to Edison's preference for (and investment in) direct current. Edison devoted every fiber of his being, the threat of his money and political influence, to block Tesla's system at all costs and to prove that AC was deadly dangerous while DC was safe—which led to the use of AC in something called the electric chair. With the backing of George Westinghouse, who bought Tesla's patents and made AC widely available, Tesla's system prevailed. By 1892,

Tesla made a triumphant lecture tour in Europe, demonstrating his system's superiority.

The Passion of Tesla

If his mind was extraordinary, so was his humanity. Tesla's story is psychologically resonant, somehow personal to everyone. Miriam Seidel centers the passion of Tesla in her libretto, bringing in his letters written to a young girl and the words of Mark Twain—but I am getting ahead of myself.

He was born during a lightning storm; lightning literally struck as he came int the world, a world where it was preordained that he was to be a priest like his father and his grandfather before him. At the age of seventeen, Tesla contracted cholera, undergoing a kind of spiritual and physical crisis. He was near death and given last rites three times. His father promised him that if he survived, he could become an engineer as he wished. He could visualize mechanical devices,

constructing and modifying them in his mind so as to route and manage electricity—which he understood to be high-frequency waves of energy. He could see this, hold it in his mind as if he held it in his hands. Electricity which passes through every language and flies across any border.

Later, having emigrated to New York, he was in effect betrayed. First by Thomas Edison, whom he worked for briefly, and then by the business partners in his first company—leaving him penniless and forcing him to work as a ditch-digger for some time. After this he transformed himself into a salesman, a showman, a performer in his own marvels. If the mention of betrayal caught your attention, this opera is for you. Opera is an artform that manifests story, music, and dance at a level of maximum intimacy and intensity.

So much about Nikola Tesla is and remains about belief, faith in the goodness of humanity upended by our failings. The opera begins with a fall: the physical fall of a great structure, Tesla's Wardenclyffe tower. That structure had embodied his monumental dream of uniting the globe through a series of multiple transmission towers, offering people around the world the promise of free, effortless, borderless communication. Fully built but never used, it was sold for scrap during World War I. In that opening scene, Jon Gibson gives voice to Tesla singing of the loss of his tower. We feel his pain and our loss that he was thwarted in giving his gift to all of us.

Even if I had many lives, I could not begin to describe what this means to me. I am, if you will indulge me, a casualty of that time, the grandson of a man hit by mustard gas in the trenches of World War I. I sat on his lap; I am sitting on it now. The greater cataclysm to optimism was not the Second World War—it was the First World War, fought entirely in Europe.

What died there was the promise of progress. Mustard gas crippled and killed thousands of conscripts on the battlefield, men who suffered respiratory distress like no more than insects. The scientific community was sickened and appalled at the un-civilizing of chemistry. Like Tesla, pioneers of aviation and other fields of science and engineering had published their patents as free open-source material, working not for wealth but in the cause of a new prosperous era for mankind. On the battlefields of that terrible war forever lay the wreckage of the collective faith in the salvation of egalitarian science. Tesla grieving the loss of his tower and its dream embodies this moment.

Radio, broadcast, wireless communication, and flying machines that would carry people across national borders and create a new world—these visions of hope were crushed. Alberto Santos-Dumont, legendary aviation pioneer and one of the richest persons in the world at that time, committed suicide when he realized that the lifework of his inventions, intended to be agents of peace, had been turned into weapons of war.

Today for so many, Tesla was a transformative figure who was too good for the world. He lived to a great age, long enough for fame to fade into obscurity. In the opera, we revisit with him the highs and lows of his experience.

Turning Tesla's story into an opera

My design was aimed at making the opera fluid and transportable. At Temple University, Sarah Drury and I began to work together on projection design with archival images that would evoke the senses of the times and of the electrical beauty of nature. Many came from the archives at the Tesla Museum, which

Performance photo: Tesla (Scott Murphree), White Dove (dancer Joanna Kotze), chorus members, and White Dove (singer, Mirjana Jovanović Stojanović), National Theater, Belgrade, July 2006. Photo by Srdjan Mihič

granted us open access. Sarah and her team traveled to Tesla's birthplace in Smiljan, Croatia and filmed the location. There, they were told that actually he was born on the road to the house. Born under the open heavens, during a lightning storm.

No, we were not in want of images. A computer-generated copy of the Nikola's tower rotated center stage; and as it is in opening movement of the text, the tower broke apart and fell to the ground. In our dress rehearsal at Temple in a happy accident, the image unexpectedly zoomed out to four or five times its size, filling the ceiling and the entire theater before falling everywhere to pieces. This spectacular image we kept. Let's break the fourth wall in the opening, shall we?

Early on after I joined the project, I knew that the White Dove—representing Tesla's mysterious friendship with a white pigeon—would be central to the opera, and how she was presented would be crucial. Preparing for the premiere in Belgrade, I realized that an idea from Noh Theater could help convey her ineffable presence to Tesla. I had seen Noh performed in Kyoto following a tour to Japan with the choreographer and dancer Simone Forti, where I also performed as a guest artist for the Trisha Brown Dance Company. We all took time off to see the arts and performances going on there. (Later on, after *Violet*

Fire closed in New York, Nina and Jon would also go to Japan to study and make work.) The idea that struck me from Noh was that the singer is present and sings in verse while the dancer embodies the character. Essentially, two people combine to make one performance—usually that of a person traveling on some kind of spiritual journey.

As soon as Nina Winthrop joined the project as choreographer, we began talking about the concept of using this Noh theatrical convention as a way to embody the dove. Nina began showing me her work in studio shortly after that. Essentially, the dancer would offer an imagining of the real pigeon so beloved by Nikola Tesla at the end of his life, while the voice of the White Dove in the soprano would suggest her connection with higher frequencies of existence. The two would merge into one being as we see so beautifully in the Noh.

Another influence on the dove's staging came from Indonesia. A play of mine, *The Bribe*, had been invited to the Singapore Arts Festival in 1994. After the festival I traveled on to Indonesia to study Wayang Parwa shadow-puppetry theater under the mentorship of master dalang I Wayan Wija. This traditional form is used to perform sacred texts from the Ramayana and Mahabharata. It divides the stage into established sectors—right and left, upper and lower quadrants, with the entrances of the various characters related to who they are in the drama of life. I brought these ideas to Belgrade, using them for the placement of Mark Twain, the Reporter, and Margaret Storm.

Performers Nenad Nenić (Reporter), Ana Lackovich (Margaret Storm), Dragana Stanković (Katharine Johnson), Miodrag Jovanović (Mark Twain) in rehearsal, National Theater, Belgrade, June 2006.

As the main character, Tesla moves everywhere, alternating across the unitary center line, as he sings about "splitting the earth like an apple," and in the penultimate scene of the opera, when he rises to depart from the stage from the upper right-hand corner, stepping off, leaving this life.

As for the dove, I placed her with her pure soprano voice in the high left-hand corner of the stage. I staged her visually floating twenty feet above the stage, and with the dancer as the Dove moving at stage level. The dancer creates the illusion that she could fly at any moment as she wordlessly addresses the figure of Tesla on the stage. Tesla, we may believe, senses her presence more than sees her. The libretto does its magic, and Mirjana Jovanović Stojanović, the soprano, sings out and across the stage as if to lift them both up into the air. Mirjana, whom everyone called Mimi because of her sensational performance as Mimi in *La Bohème*, sang pure long notes without vibrato—both in a nod to Jon's work as an instrumentalist, and to bring a free open voice to the figure of the Dove.

Before the premiere, we convened for several weeks of rehearsals with the Serbian singers, dancers, and musicians in Belgrade. In rehearsal Nina Winthrop was able to work with the dancers using recordings that Jon made with the New Music Orchestra (NMO), a group in Katowice, Poland entirely dedicated to contemporary music. While planning for the premiere, we had decided to move from a nine-member chamber orchestra as we had at Temple University (played by the Relâche Ensemble) to the bigger sound of a twelve-member orchestra. It was a significant upgrade, and Jon loved the fuller dimension of the sound. Thanks to Merilyn Jackson's extensive network of artistic contacts in Poland, we arranged for NMO to perform the score at a time that Jon was on tour in Europe with Philip Glass, and could get over to Katowice during a break. All this arranged, I traveled there to meet the group and join the recording.

When rehearsals began eight months later in Belgrade, we were able to play the recording with the singers and dancers. Those sections where the Dove appeared to Tesla really got into our bones. Joanna Kotze was the primary dancer, with Kristen Hollinsworth as her second. In performance, Nina had Kristen doubling Joanna (another doubling), such that Joanna would disappear from Tesla and Kristen immediately appear—creating, in effect, a live jump cut.

The White Dove appeared at crucial moments throughout the opera, with Mirjana/Mimi appearing floating high above the stage out of the darkness and her voice presaging the entrance of the dancer. Nina choreographed intuitively within these parameters. This all-important figure in the libretto was fully formed in studio and was perhaps the most carefully prepared element in the opera by the time the New York artists arrived to join the Serbian singers and orchestra for rehearsals in the week before Tesla's 150th birthday celebration.

Our set and costume designer Boris Čakširan gave me five full-length, ten-meter-high shifting panels standing right and left, offering us precise flat surfaces for Sarah Drury's projections. Boris called these screens "the brothers," a perfect ground for the exact shaping of the projections that seemed to be painted on the screens as they moved, and in the next moment effortlessly changing with the music. Lighting designer Mary Louise Geiger, a longtime collaborator from the US, managed to intensify the projection with her work which would swell and take the stage like music.

Ana Zorana Brajovič (left) and Terry O'Reilly in rehearsal for Violet Fire, *National Theater, Belgrade, June 2006*

For the chorus, I clustered them as a unit, merging strolling pigeon movements with the sense of the voice of the *polis* singing, out of Greek theater. Boris designed their costumes to make them more than human personas, and flocked them in pigeon hues—which at times could make sixteen appear to be many more. The impeccable Ivana Dragutinović Maričić, opera director for the Belgrade National Theater, fine-tuned the choral movement, making them a powerful unhurried force. They could seem to be permanent and then be gone. In one scene, the chorus sang entirely off stage with close-packed voices placing their unmistakably live presence into the atmosphere of the stage. My direction to them was: louder. I recall Jon particularly enjoying that choice, saying the audience can see them and not see them in the same moment.

When I first arrived in Belgrade, conductor Ana Zorana Brajović and her mother Ljiljanka Brajović, a nationally famous surgeon and voice specialist, welcomed me into their home. Ana and I shared our appreciation of this new opera, of the libretto and the transcending minimalism and lyricism of Jon's music. Conductors are far more important in opera than directors—they cue the singers in performance, and this bond is absolute. At Ana's direction we added two stands of violins, expanding the orchestra from twelve to twenty musicians. Together we assembled our cast of singers, led by the incomparable Scott Murphree, who brought a beautiful tenor voice and an actor's understanding of Tesla to the role. Darko Đorđević also sang the role brilliantly in Belgrade and for our invited dress rehearsal in New York.

My conscious blending of Eastern and Western forms throughout the opera, bringing in values of the Noh theater and Indonesian shadow puppetry with western staging, was very much in line with Serbian artists' life and worldview. Through time and in the present day, the people look to the East as they simultaneously see the West: a Janus culture. I came to appreciate this as a secret weapon in the performance. It became an intangible presence to better understand who Tesla was and why he is so revered.

What Tesla gives us

Tesla could make you proud to be human. A deeply spiritual man, his gifts he gave away. His many patents were not only records of a far-reaching imagination; they were guidebooks for others to use. He made fortunes, and then spent them on his experimental work. He was ultimately motivated by the desire to gift humanity with his transformative inventions, helping to improve people's lives.

As a scientist, Tesla makes us ask the question: who owns the deed to an idea? If someone buys an idea, that buyer takes nominal ownership. And yet we see that so much of our wireless world with its ever-present alternating current and thousands of other inventions we daily use, these will always be gifts from Tesla's great mind. The passage from the maker to the user is a pattern as old as humankind; it is how this is managed that defines us, and marks us in time. I see Tesla as restoring an older tradition, one that predates capitalism and harks back to gift economies. This radical traditionalism offers us a hope for the future, at least as strong as Tesla's profusion of inventions.

Terry O'Reilly directed all productions of Violet Fire. *A playwright, performer and director, and longtime co-artistic director of Mabou Mines, he has worked internationally in Japan, Indonesia, Thailand, China, Hong Kong, Taipei, Nanning, Rio de Janeiro, Singapore, Western Europe, the Czech Republic, Poland, and Serbia and Montenegro. More under Collaborators in the Appendix.*

VIOLET FIRE: A DANCE CRITIC'S VIEW

Merilyn Jackson

Although we had only a little to do with *Violet Fire*, my husband, Arthur Sabatini, and I watched its development with interest. We had a decades-long connection with Miriam Seidel—more about that later. And she and I had worked side by side as dance critics for the *Philadelphia Inquirer* for some years in the nineties and the early 2000s. There was by then more to cover than one writer could handle, and rather than becoming rivals, we bonded with each other over pitching the companies we wanted to review, and collaborating on scheduling. Miriam didn't care much for writing about the ballet, for example, so I took that over.

So it shouldn't have been a surprise to find out that in her opera project, dance played a strong role among the other elements of the multimedia production. All of this ignited my interest and involvement in seeing *Violet Fire* light up the stage for its first performance at Temple University's Tomlinson Theater, with Terry O'Reilly directing a cast of student singers. While we loved hearing Jon Gibson's glamorous, nearly mystical score for this opera about Nikola Tesla's electric life, I couldn't help imagining how a full professional production would elevate the show. So when I learned that *Violet Fire* would be part of the Next Wave Festival at the Brooklyn Academy of Music in 2006, after its world premiere at the National Theater of Belgrade, I wanted to write a preview focusing on its dance elements.

White Dove (dancer, Joanna Kotze), Violet Fire, *Scene 3, National Theater, Belgrade, July 2006*

I already knew that the dancers took the part of Tesla's beloved pigeons, making them central to the opera. The *Inquirer*'s music critic, David Patrick Stearns, had written about the opera, but had not had much to say about the dancers, all Temple students—Milsy Davis took the role of the White Dove, while Cynthia St. Clair, Jocelyn Isaac, and Jennifer Rose danced the pigeons. Philip Grosser choreographed.

Here is how the article I wrote for *Exploredance.com* began:

> If you swoon over the story of a man falling in love with a swan, then you may also be enthralled by the story of a man who falls in love with a dove, or, if you like, a pigeon. But while *Swan Lake* is a fairy tale, the tale of

White Dove (dancer, Joanna Kotze), Violet Fire, *Scene 2, National Theater, Belgrade, July 2006*

revolutionary inventor and thinker, Nikola Tesla and his love for a pigeon, which became his muse, is real. His story, as told by librettist Miriam Seidel, composer Jon Gibson, director Terry O'Reilly (co-artistic director of Mabou Mines) and choreographer Nina Winthrop, in a multi-media opera called *Violet Fire* is the stuff of fairy tales.

Issues around the choreography, the set and the costumes, had all been addressed in advance of the world premiere on July 10, 2006 at The National Theater of Belgrade. The production was to be part of the celebration of the 150th anniversary of Tesla's birth at the BELEF Summer Arts Festival. Nina Winthrop, who would later marry Jon Gibson, had been invited to create the new, tender, mysterious choreography. Nina had studied with Erick Hawkins, Merce Cunningham and Deborah Hay and started her own company, Nina Winthrop and Dancers in 1991.

Here's much of the interview from the Exploredance.com piece with Winthrop, who worked with Joanna Kotze (of the Wally Cardona Quartet) to create what promised to be an alluring, and possibly, alarming pigeon.

"About three months after the Philadelphia workshop, I heard from Terry (O'Reilly). He invited me onto the project," she said. "I had been to the workshop and was drawn to the work at first because of Jon's music." When given the chance to choreograph for it she said, "From the beginning though, Miriam's libretto was really my guiding force."

"I knew it was going to be a solo and Terry asked me to create movement for specific scenes following the story line, although the Dove is always onstage when the singer is."

Once she cast Kotze in the role, the two went out to study pigeon movement. "I work from improvisation with my dancers and a lot came from Joanna. I would give her floor patterns to follow. We worked with [the patterns of] alternating currents, the infinity sign and circles in the dance phrases. The dance phrase in the first scene is the infinity sign," she said. [Merce Cunningham, by the way, was into bird movement, and also created a dance based on his observations.]

"The music is almost romantic," Winthrop said, "rather than minimalist, and Joanna goes off of beats but not all the time. It's more of a mood setter and a general timing setting."

At one point she had another dancer, Kristen Hollinsworth, do a very similar flight across the stage a second after one of Kotze's, almost like a blurred vision of the first. "But they are never on stage at the same time," she said, adding that she hopes it contributes to the mystical qualities of the work.

It did. The loving makeover by the staff at the National Theater of Belgrade, including enthralling new costumes and sets designed by Boris Čakširan and produced in house, all allowed O'Reilly's vision of the stagecraft to blossom. Months later, it was a huge success at The Brooklyn Academy of Music. Yet it has never been remounted in Philadelphia or elsewhere. And that is something that, in my opinion, really should happen.

Interconnections

Violet Fire was not by any means the only adventurous artistic project to come out of Philadelphia, often challenging the city's larger ivory-tower cultural institutions. The Philadelphia Ballet (founded as the Pennsylvania Ballet) stepped out into the streets during the AIDs crisis, its dancers choreographing and performing in the annual *Shut up And Dance* benefits. Companies like the Relâche Ensemble challenged the status quo of the orchestra, and Headlong Dance Company, the Ballet, Pig Iron Theater and the Wilma offered tastier shows than the staid Broadway touring gruel Philly audiences fed on. Gallery spaces for visual arts and new media work offered similarly innovative fare.

The opera grew in an atmosphere of collaboration and sometimes surprising interconnections occurring among different parts of the arts community. For *Violet Fire*, Temple University offered a productive first collaboration with faculty and students in various departments, as well as with Relâche, an ensemble devoted to new music. Longtime director and Mabou Mines co-artistic director, Terry O'Reilly (also an actor and a former dancer), staged the opera brilliantly, if on a shoestring, and the show was critically well received in Philadelphia. (Mabou Mines has a long history with Philip Glass, a founding member of Mabou.)

My friendship with Miriam goes back to the 1980s, when my husband, Arthur Sabatini, was involved in the production of a series at Yellow Springs Institute in rural Chester County, Pennsylvania, called *Six Saturdays*. I was handling publicity for The Relâche Ensemble. This is where Miriam, who spoke at one of the events, says she first heard Relâche. It may have been a performance, or even a premiere, of Pauline Oliveros' *The Well*, a Relâche commission.

One Saturday we recall was an afternoon with theatre and performance scholar Richard Schechner, for which I made a timballo, an overstuffed pasta dish, meant to reference his theory of the seven functions of performance. As we sat around the picnic blanket cutting and serving it, I pointed out to Richard that I had made it with seven layers. He counted the layers inside as he began to eat and noted there were only six. I told him, the seventh is the structure, the crust

White Dove (dancer, Joanna Kotze),
Violet Fire, Scene 5, National Theater,
Belgrade, 2006

holding it all together, and you are eating it. I recall the glance he shot my way. Miriam took part in a huge ritual event while she was a student at Swarthmore, which she remembers being directed by a young Richard Schechner. Another memorable experience from that time, expanding her sense of theatrical possibilities, was hearing the Sun Ra Arkestra play at a West Philadelphia club. "That was a multimedia gesammtkunstwerk—wall of sound, African robes, tin-foil crowns and all," she recalls.

Miriam and I stayed in contact now and then even after Arthur and I moved to Phoenix, where he would teach and cofound the Interdisciplinary Arts Department at Arizona State University. When Miriam was developing *Violet Fire*, Arthur enthusiastically recommended Terry as a director. We had seen him in action when he had a residency at ASU as a principal with Mabou Mines, part of a multi-year program with the legendary theater company, along with the late Lee Breuer,

Fred Neumann and Ruth Maleczech. Terry's entry into the project became another one of those magical artistic interconnections.

The conceptual artist Lowry Burgess was another Yellow Springs guest. Miriam was fascinated by his work and ended up writing about him for a number of publications including the *Philadelphia Inquirer*. In one article, for the *New Art Examiner*, she wrote, "'Like good science fiction writers, he offers us valuable practice in the imagining of vast distances and exotic processes." When we talked about this recently, she added, "You could say that about Tesla also." Back then, I hadn't known about Miriam's interest in science fiction, which goes back to her childhood. "I'd say that the same things that drew me to SFF also attracted me to Tesla," she told me.

Everyone involved in this project, from Seidel to O'Reilly, Winthrop, and the late Jon Gibson made good bedfellows. But Miriam and I have yet one other interconnection: Andrei Codrescu. While she went to writing workshops with him, he published a dozen or so of my poems. Nothing delights me more than seeing Andrei's poem about Tesla here and being between the same sheets with him and Miriam and her libretto. Because as the critic John Perreault said in a review of *Violet Fire* on the online *ArtsJournal*, "The surprise for me is not that Seidel's libretto bounces around in time—adding to the man-outside-of-time theme—but that it is poetry."

Merilyn Jackson has written on dance for the Philadelphia Inquirer since 1996 and writes on dance, theater, food, travel, Eastern European culture, and Latin American fiction for publications including the New York Times, the Warsaw Voice, the Arizona Republic, Phoenix New Times, MIT's Technology Review, Arizona Highways, Dance, Pointe and Dance Teacher magazines, and Broad Street Review. She currently writes for Fjord and tanz magazin, Berlin. She was awarded an NEA Critics Fellowship in 2005 to Duke University and a Pennsylvania Council on the Arts Fellowship for her novel-in-progress, Solitary Host.

CONDUCTING NIKOLA TESLA'S OPERA

Ana Zorana Brajović

Working on *Violet Fire* opened some new visions of opera to me. For me, before seeing this wonderful score, opera was a perfect form of expression with the largest possible ensemble. My first glance at the score was a surprise—I found the beauty and depth in the simplicity of those beautiful and catchy melodies. The libretto offered a mixture of sadness and loneliness, honesty, and joy of creation. In my line of work as in Tesla's, when working on and studying a project, you are alone, and the process separates you from the real world. Sometimes you get baffled and scared by the crowd that is waiting for you when you open the door of your practice room—or in Tesla's case, his laboratory. It was easy to find the same language with the libretto because of those similarities.

Working with Jon and Terry was so much fun for the whole ensemble. Their vast knowledge of Nikola Tesla and his life (he is our hero, not theirs) could only spark great admiration for the foreigners who really dove into the psychology of our (and now we can say one of the world's) greatest scientists.

I still talk to the doves in the park and discuss the hardest life decisions I have to make... somehow it seems they can help. I feel I understand Tesla that way. To this day, the singers who were part of the performances of *Violet Fire* still remember the song of the pigeons, and they sing it when I enter the practice

Ana Zorana Brajović conducting the orchestra of the National Theater, Belgrade, in rehearsals for Violet Fire, *June 2006*

rooms. My biggest regret is that it didn't stay longer on the repertoire of the National Theater; I think it would have had a long stage life.

Tesla was a hero, a dreamer, and a wizard, and *Violet Fire* was a perfect representation of his struggles and his dilemmas.

Ana Zorana Brajović (Conductor) is Opera Director at the National Theater of Belgrade. She has received the annual October Award, the highest award in Belgrade for music achievement. For the National Theater Opera House in Belgrade, she has conducted the operas of Mozart, Verdi, Puccini, Rossini, Bizet, Donizetti, Strauss and others. More under Collaborators in the Appendix.

VIOLET FIRE: THE LIBRETTO

VIOLET FIRE
An opera about Nikola Tesla

Music: Jon Gibson
Libretto: Miriam Seidel

with portions adapted to music by Jon Gibson

CAST

NIKOLA TESLA, born Croatia 1856, died New York City, 1943 (tenor)

REPORTER (baritone)

WHITE DOVE (soprano)

KATHARINE JOHNSON, Tesla's closest woman friend
        (mezzo-soprano)

MARK TWAIN, a friend of Tesla (bass baritone)

MARGARET STORM, author of "Return of the Dove," positing Tesla's
        extraterrestrial origin (contralto)

CHORUS

PIGEONS

Summary by Scene

Scene 1 (Prologue)

Nikola Tesla mourns the loss of Wardenclyffe, his massive tower on Long Island. The tower, meant to be the first in a planned World Broadcasting System, had stood vacant since J.P. Morgan withdrew funding, and was finally demolished in 1917. The tower's loss means the end of Tesla's grand dream of providing a global network of communication and free energy.

Scene 2

Bryant Park, New York, 1922, late at night: A reporter tells how the "Great Inventor" can now be found on park benches, feeding pigeons. Tesla's great achievements in alternating current, radio, phosphorescent light, and robotics might be behind him, but he's still good for a quote about the future. Tesla's beloved White Dove approaches. They sing together, recalling his moments of communion with the inner secrets of nature that led to his greatest discoveries.

Scene 3

Tesla's hotel apartment / Katharine Johnson's parlor, New York, 1920s: Tesla and Katharine are caught in parallel reveries. She yearns to reach him, by "thought transference" if necessary, to touch the humanity of her elusive, "dear and silent" friend. He slips into another duet with the White Dove, remembering his lifelong search along the path of higher frequencies.

Scene 4

Tesla's laboratory in downtown New York (decades earlier). Tesla puts on a stunning display of electrical marvels for the press and the public. Mark Twain gives voice to the awe felt by the crowd (Chorus) at the sprays of electricity and mysterious glowing lights—as if Tesla had Godlike powers, turning night into day, fulfilling some Manifest Destiny by subduing nature.

Margaret Storm and Katharine Johnson enter Tesla's memory of this peak of his fame and glory, offering dueling visions of his achievements: Storm views Tesla as an unearthly being, sent to Earth to lift humanity to a new stage, while Johnson wants only to save his human legacy. The White Dove returns, pulling the crowd to contemplate the "blinding light" that beckoned Tesla forward throughout his life.

Scene 5

Bryant Park (1920s) / Tesla's reverie. The Reporter recalls some of Tesla's more outlandish predictions: power sent by radio, turning the Earth into a gigantic dynamo. Margaret Storm continues to rhapsodize over Tesla, while Katharine, in despair, now warns of the destructive consequences of Tesla's work through exposure to altered frequencies. While Tesla protests that he just wanted to help end human suffering, the White Dove enacts this suffering and dies.

Scene 6
Tesla's hotel apartment, New York, 1943. Tesla recalls his first encounter with electricity, as a small child on his family's farm, when he stroked the cat and saw "a sheet of light" around his hand. The three women (Johnson, Storm, White Dove) encourage him to "lay down the fire" and let go. Tesla and the White Dove, reunited, ascend.

Notes on the libretto

Two direct quotations appear in the text:

Scene 2: J. W. von Goethe, passage from *Faust*. Tesla related that this passage came to him at the moment of his discovery of the rotating magnetic field, making possible alternating-current electrical induction.

Scene 4: Mark Twain, from *Letters from the Earth*.

Margaret Storm's metaphysical work *Return of the Dove* (1959) is the source from which her lines are adapted.

Much of the Reporter's lines are from actual newspaper headlines and articles.

Katharine Johnson's lines in Scene 3 are adapted from Katharine Johnson's letters to Tesla.

The White Dove's lines are inspired in part by passages from Tesla's *Colorado Springs Notes*.

A letter written by Tesla near the end of his life to a young girl, Pola Fotic, is the source of the beginning of Scene 6.

Score for Violet Fire *by Jon Gibson, p. 29, Scene 1, "My tower...," Courtesy Estate of Jon Gibson*

SCENE 1

PROLOGUE:
WARDENCLYFFE, LONG ISLAND, circa 1917

TESLA stands center stage. He is tall, formally dressed in dark suit and white shirt.

Seen in images: Wardenclyffe Tower: a mushroom-domed tower structure, like a UFO on stilts. The tower goes online: lightning streams from its dome, the stage is flooded with rhythmic BURSTS OF LIGHT.

A series of explosive BOOMS, the tower disappears. TESLA paces the stage, *in extremis*.

> TESLA

> Perhaps I was a little
> Premature, perhaps
> Too far ahead of time
> My tower

> "The transmission of electrical
> energy without wires as a
> means of furthering peace"

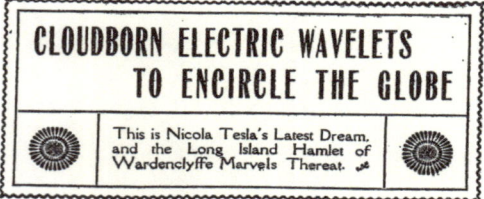

Top left: Wardenclyffe Tower and station, Shoreham, Long Island, 1904

Top right: Performance photo from Violet Fire, *Scene 1, Tesla (Scott Murphree) against image of electrical diagram, National Theater, Belgrade, July 2006. Photo by Srdjan Mihič*

Above left: Headline of article about Tesla's Wardenclyffe tower project, from New York Times, *March 27, 1904*

All ready to transmit
Switch it on, and broadcast
Signals through the earth
Power through the earth
Glowing lines of energy
Undulating through
Undulating through
Flowing through the
Cool, dark earth
Lightning through the synapses
Earth becomes a single brain
My tower
Distance means nothing
End to end
Brain to brain
Mind to mind
No loss of intensity

Projection image from Violet Fire, *Scene 1: composite image of electrical diagram and Tesla's pigeon*

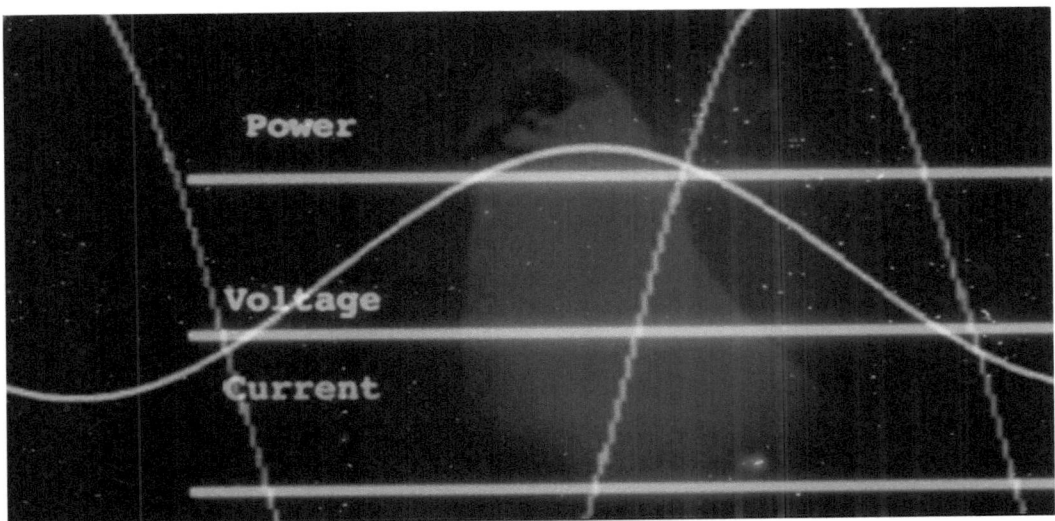

Point to point
Mind to mind
Heart to heart
Now the bones lie in the grass
Sea breeze whistling through the ruins
Perhaps I was a little
Premature, perhaps
Too far ahead of time
My tower

(repeats from "The transmission of electricity...")

End SCENE 1.

Score for Violet Fire by Jon Gibson, p. 9, Scene 2, Part 1, "At night and in secret...," Courtesy Estate of Jon Gibson

SCENE 2

NEW YORK CITY, 1922

TESLA remains on stage, REPORTER enters. STAGEHANDS
bring out park bench. Suggestion of TWINKLING CITY LIGHTS
AND STARS in background.

REPORTER pulls out a notepad. During the following, TESLA
takes a small bag from his pocket, throws seed as PIGEONS
approach him.

REPORTER

> At night and in secret
> Nikola Tesla lavishes his love on pigeons
> Midnight is the hour of his visits
> Every midnight for the last five years
> He calls them down to where he stands
> Scatters the seed on the grass
> The old G.I., we used to call him—
> Great Inventor—hasn't come up with much
> Since ninety-nine or before
> His tower sold for scrap (repeats)
> So much for World Broadcasting

For Five Years Electrical Genius Has Fed Birds
at Public Library and Carried the Injured Away
for Best Treatment Wealth and Skill Can Provide

GUARDIAN ANGEL OF PIGEONS

They say the lights around here
All run on his system.
Alternating current—he came up with that.
'Far superior to Edison's approach,'
He says. Then why is Edison so famous,
And he's here scattering seed at night?
He's always good for a line
Can't follow all that he says
If half of it were true
We'd be living like Buck Rogers
By nineteen twenty-nine.

Midnight is the hour of his visits
Every midnight for the last five years
He calls them down to where he stands
Scatters the seed on the grass
At night and in secret.
At night and in secret
Nikola Tesla lavishes his love
on pigeons.

*Above: Headline and illustration for article
about Tesla feeding pigeons,* New York
World, *November 21, 1926*

Below: Performance photo from Violet Fire,
*Scene 2, Tesla (Scott Murphree) against
image of trees and park bench, National
Theater, Belgrade, July 2006.
Photo by Srdjan Mihič*

REPORTER exits. WHITE DOVE enters. TESLA
regards her with careful wonder.

WHITE DOVE
What is your wish
(Sings wordlessly)

TESLA is entranced. Through the following, CITY
LIGHTS are replaced by suggestions of STARS,
ELECTRON TRAILS, etc.

TESLA
Who are you

       WHITE DOVE
       Endless
       Endless horizon

TESLA
Dear Heart
Dear Heart

       WHITE DOVE
       Atoms
       Atoms weaving

TESLA
Precious
Precious

       WHITE DOVE
       Etheric filaments
       Atoms weaving lines
         of force

TESLA
Perfect
Precious

NURSING SICK BIRDS IS INVENTOR'S HOBBY

Tesla Cares for Pigeons When Not Making Designs for Niagara Power Plant.

CRUMBS ATTRACT THEM

Scientist Sends 'Patients' to a Bird Hospital, It Is Learned as S. P. C. A. Opens New Annex.

Above: Projection image from *Violet Fire*, Scene 2: composite image including historic view of Bryant Park, New York, and tree branches

Below: Headline for article about Tesla feeding pigeons, New York Times, April 15, 1927

Performance photo from Violet Fire, *Scene 2: White Dove (dancer, Joanna Kotze) and White Dove (singer, Mirjana Jovanović Stojanović), National Theater, Belgrade, July 2006. Photo by Srdjan Mihič*

WHITE DOVE
Long nights

WHITE DOVE
Long nights riding
Magnetic lines of force
Spinning in the dynamo
Come with me (repeats)

TESLA
Yes, so hard to sleep

TESLA
I remember
Spinning lines of force
One inside the other
You flew in there.

The fields spun free
So easily, no friction
A new way to make
Electricity.

I saw it clearly
Before it was made
New on this earth
And you flew inside.
I was not alone
You were with me
At the moment
Of discovery
We flew inside.

TESLA/WHITE DOVE
We flew inside (repeats)
inside (repeats)

Large spinning CIRCLES of light glow on, moving in background.
MUSIC.

TESLA/WHITE DOVE

"The sun dips down, the day is spent

Rushing below, she must begin again (repeats)

There is no wing to lift me from the ground

To follow always higher toward the sun!

A shining dream! Even as light pales

So sad, the wings of spirit are no help

To lift this body up by wings of flesh."

(repeats from "The sun dips down...")

There is no wing to lift me from the ground

LIGHTS/PROJECTIONS fade. End SCENE 2.

Projection image from Violet Fire,
*Scene 2: composite image, Tesla's patent
diagram for Electric Magnetic Motor,
superimposed on image of sky*

Score for Violet Fire *by Jon Gibson, p. 102, Scene 3, "Please let me hear a word," Courtesy Estate of Jon Gibson*

SCENE 3

TESLA'S HOTEL APARTMENT. TESLA and WHITE DOVE
remain on stage. KATHARINE JOHNSON enters, wearing long
evening dress.

KATHARINE JOHNSON
The candles have burned low
The cognac must be poured
The conversation slows
You never come to dinner anymore.
I wish I could have news of you
My dear and silent friend
I would be happy if I knew
Something about you. You,
Who have no human needs.
This is not what I wanted to say.
Send me a thought and
It will be received.
This is not what I wanted to say.

TESLA does not acknowledge her. KATHARINE turns her back
on TESLA.

Performance photo from Violet Fire, *Scene 3: l-r,*
Katharine Johnson (Dragana Stanković),
Tesla (Darko Dordević). Photo by Srdjan Mihič

TESLA

High frequency
Phenomena from
My apparatus:
Luminous clouds
Mysterious rays
Excited electrons
Cold fire, flames
That do not consume:
The beating of wings
The beating of wings
The beating of wings

As he sings, he picks up a fluorescent tube that comes on at his touch. Through the following, COILS switch on one by one, sparks winding or leaping like little lightning bolts, BUZZING and ZAPPING. In background, LIGHTNING-LIKE COIL EFFECTS are mirrored and amplified in projection.

Left: Performance photo from Violet Fire, *Scene 3: l-r, Tesla (Darko Dordević), White Dove (dancer, Joanna Kotze). Photo by Srdjan Mihič*

Below: Projection image from Violet Fire, *Scene 3: composite image of electrical diagrams representing Tesla's work*

WHITE DOVE
All vibration

TESLA
Higher frequencies

WHITE DOVE
Oscillation

TESLA
Tongues of living flame

WHITE DOVE
No cessation

TESLA
The beating of wings
The beating of wings
The beating of wings

He touches COIL, becoming a living conductor of electricity.
Virtual LIGHTNING shoots from his hand.

TESLA/WHITE DOVE

In resonance
Perfect resonance
Touch the fire
The finer fibers
Finely tuned
Touch the fire (repeats)
(MUSIC)

TESLA

Leap the gap
Touch my heart

He steps away from coils, moves to WHITE DOVE.
KATHARINE turns again toward TESLA. Background effects
subdue.

KATHARINE

My dear and silent friend
Sometimes I want to tell you
What I know about thought
Transference. I call it that
For want of a better word.
I have often wished and meant
To speak to you of this
But when I am with you
I never say the things I intended to say.
You do not know what you need.

TESLA

Mother—

KATHARINE

No! You do not know what you need

TESLA

Mother, please

> I miss you
> I need to touch (repeats)

She seems not to notice him.

> KATHARINE
> Send me a thought, and
> It will be received

She retreats. Background effects back, STRONGER than before.

> TESLA
> (agitated)
> Leap the gap
> Collapse the distance
> Wireless transmission
> Heart to heart!
> Circuits in resonance

> WHITE DOVE
> Curving trails

TESLA
Ground the transmitter

WHITE DOVE
Ride the crests

TESLA
Circuits in resonance
Distance disappears

WHITE DOVE
Soaring
Ride the airwaves

KATHARINE
(lying down on bench)
I wish I could have word of you
My dear and silent friend

Performance photo from Violet Fire, *Scene 3: l-r,*
Tesla (Scott Murphree), Katharine Johnson
(Dragana Stanković). Photo by Srdjan Mihič

Detached from all but memory,
I am filled with sadness
And long for that which is not.
Please let me hear a word
I feel as if everything in life
Had slipped away from me
Please let me hear a word
Please let me hear a word
Please let me hear a word from you
    (closes her eyes)

              TESLA

  Broadcast
    (repeats)

End SCENE 3.

Projection image from Violet Fire, *Scene 3: composite image of engraving representing Wardenclyffe Tower from stationery for Tesla Company Inc., 8 West 40th Street, New York, c. 1900, against field of stars*

Score for Violet Fire *by Jon Gibson, p. 41, Scene 4, "In all these trying splendors," Courtesy Estate of Jon Gibson*

Tesla's Opera

SCENE 4

PARK, but also TESLA'S LABORATORY, where he demonstrated electrical marvels for the press and the public.

TESLA center stage. MARK TWAIN, KATHARINE JOHNSON, REPORTER, MARGARET STORM (in fifties suit), WHITE DOVE, CHORUS, are onstage all raptly watching TESLA.

To MUSIC, he raises his hands with a magician's poise, making different COILS turn on in turn, rising and subsiding to his gestures. Interspersed with his actions:

> REPORTER
>> How did he do that?
>> He says it's good for you.
>> One hundred thousand volts
>> It may be dangerous!
>> It must be dangerous!

As other effects including projections respond to his hands:

> CHORUS, ALL EXCEPT TESLA
> (repeats REPORTER'S words, above)

Portrait of Nikola Tesla holding a wireless light bulb,
by Sarony, original for a cover illustration for
the Electrical Experimenter, *1919*

TESLA holds out his hand, where a luminous globe appears. He holds it aloft, his face catching its glow. As it fades, we see BLUE FILAMENTS arcing from his fingertips.

           ALL EXCEPT TESLA
Ah!

Applause. TWAIN stands, inspired.

        TWAIN
    "He lifted his hand, and from it
    burst a fountain-spray of fire

              ALL EXCEPT TESLA
        Ah!

        TWAIN
    "A million stupendous suns

              ALL EXCEPT TESLA
        Ah!

Projection image from Violet Fire, *Scene 3: composite image of electrical discharge against field of stars*

                    TWAIN
"which clove the blackness
and soared

                              ALL EXCEPT TESLA
                    Ah!

                    TWAIN
"away and away and away

                              ALL EXCEPT TESLA
                    Ah!

                    TWAIN
"diminishing in magnitude and intensity

                              ALL EXCEPT TESLA
                    Ah!

                    TWAIN
"as they pierced the far frontiers
of space

                              ALL EXCEPT TESLA
                    Ah!

Illustration of Nikola Tesla illuminated by electrical discharges, accompanying interview with him in New York World, July 22, 1894. Original caption: "Showing the Inventor in the Effulgent Glory of Myriad Tongues of Electric Flame After He Has Saturated Himself with Electricity"

TWAIN
"until at last they were but
as diamond nailheads sparkling
under the domed vast roof of the universe."
And that was just his early career.

ALL EXCEPT TESLA
Ah!

TWAIN
I only make them laugh

ALL EXCEPT TESLA
Ha Ha Ha Ha!

TWAIN
He horrifies them

ALL EXCEPT TESLA
Ah!

TWAIN
With his blinding visions.

ALL EXCEPT TESLA
Ah! Ah! Ah! (Repeats)

TESLA/CHORUS
Resonance yields amplification
Great effects from small vibration
Fill the skies with ionization
Who will see the transformation

ALL EXCEPT TESLA
Ah! Ah! Ah! (Repeats)

In projection, IMAGES of INFERNAL MACHINES, SMOKE,
BLUEPRINTS emerge and disappear.

TWAIN
Prodigious sums of energy
From the powers of invention

TESLA/CHORUS
One hundred million volts

CHORUS
Ah Ah Ah!

TWAIN
Great shows of force
Man will have dominion

CHORUS
Ah Ah Ah!

TESLA
One hundred million volts

TESLA/CHORUS
Fountain sprays of fire
Tidal waves through earth
Electrify the earth

CHORUS
Ah Ah Ah!

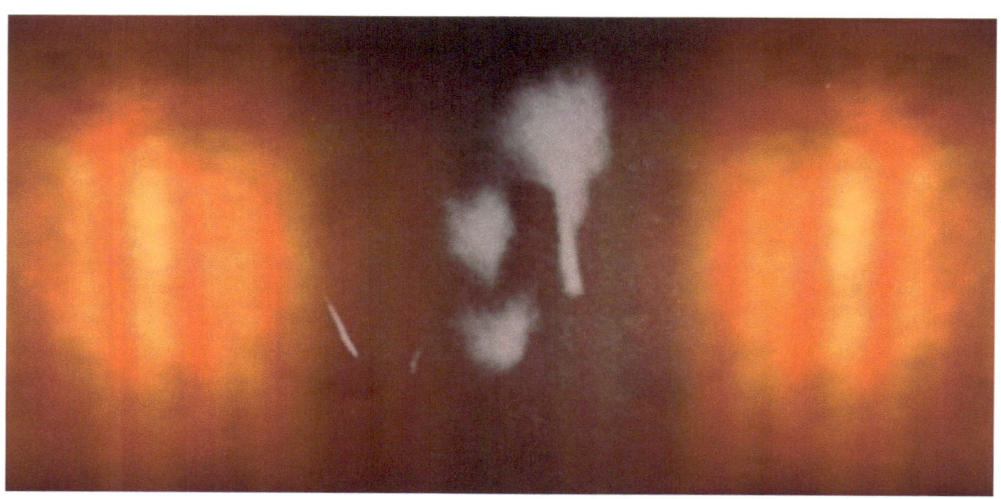

Projection image from Violet Fire, *Scene 4: composite image of Nikola Tesla, from 1894 photograph of Tesla in his laboratory, said to be first photograph taken by phosphorescent light, against pulsing bars of light*

TWAIN
Cities of brilliant light
The wizard with his wand
Will have dominion

CHORUS
Ah Ah Ah!

TESLA/CHORUS
Resonance yields amplification
Great effects from small vibration
Fill the skies with ionization
Who will see the transformation

CHORUS
Ah Ah Ah Ah Ah!
The cloudless skies receive
This strange blue light

TESLA/CHORUS
Ionize the upper atmospheres
Charge the smallest particles

TWAIN
Fire the torpedoes
Throw 'em full speed ahead!

TESLA
Charge the smallest particles

TESLA/CHORUS
Fill the glowing clouds
A strange blue light
All over the sky

CHORUS
Ah! Ah! Ah!

TWAIN
Endless lights will modify
The darkness of our nights!

CHORUS
Ah! Ah! Ah!

TESLA/CHORUS
Further use of oscillation
Greatest force from least vibration

CHORUS
Ah! Ah Ah Ah Ah!

TWAIN
Behold this horrible weaponry
Will force man into harmony

CHORUS
Ha Ha Ha Ha Ha!

TESLA
Oscillate the globe
Throw rivers from their beds
The highest buildings fall

CHORUS
Ah! Ah Ah Ah Ah! (Repeats)

TESLA
A mass of tangled stone will
Heave up the shaking land
I can split the earth
Like an apple!

I can split the earth
Like an apple!
I can split the earth
Like an apple!

CHORUS
Ah! Ah! Ah!

TWAIN
Disturb the cosmic order
Frighten the damn human race

CHORUS
Ah! Ah! Ah!

TWAIN
Into peace.

CHORUS
Ha ha ha!

TWAIN
In all these trying splendors

CHORUS
Ah! Ah! Ah!

TWAIN & CHORUS
You will have dominion
You will have dominion
You will have dominion

CHORUS
Ah! (Repeats)

MARGARET STORM steps forward. Through the following,
TESLA puts his attention elsewhere, while TWAIN reacts to
her words.

MARGARET STORM
Prince of the Violet Fire

Performance photo from Violet Fire,
*Scene 4: l-r, Tesla (Scott Murphree),
Katharine Johnson (Dragana Stanković),
Mark Twain (Miodrag Jovanović),
Reporter (Nenad Nenić), Chorus member.
Photo by Srdjan Mihič*

TWAIN
A Lady admirer!

STORM
Lord of the Seventh Ray

TWAIN
Lord, save us from adoration.

STORM
The Seventh Ray, the
Violet Fire of Venus
Emissary from the Second Planet!
Born in the Fourth Ether
Visitor from higher realms
The endless blueness of space
You, Adept and Initiate
Have come to this dark star
With angelic entities
In the bodies of doves.

TWAIN
Must have took a wrong turn
This side of Halley's comet.

Above: Projection image from Violet Fire, *Scene 4: composite image of Tesla's pigeon, vintage light bulb, banks of electric lights*

Below: Performance photo from Violet Fire, *Scene 4: l-r, Reporter (Nenad Nenić), Margaret Storm (Ana Lacković), Chorus members. Photo by Srdjan Mihič*

STORM

Minister to our vibrations
Prepare us for initiation
Into cosmic freedom.
Tune our finer fibers
Raise our subtle bodies
Bring the cleansing fire,
The violet flame.
O Visitor from starry space
Prince of the violet fire
Come to me on healing wings of peace
Light the flame within my heart.

KATHARINE steps between MARGARET STORM and MARK
TWAIN, agitated.

KATHARINE

No! You cannot see
In his hidden heart, hear his secret thoughts.
He only wants to touch
To make a world for us, the brightest
Future, peace, things you can't imagine
No one will listen, can't you explain
        (to TESLA)
Tell them!
Tell me!

WHITE DOVE moves forward. TESLA listens closely to the
following, moves closer to her.

WHITE DOVE

Flying through moonlight
Pulsing stars
Etheric filaments weaving

WHITE DOVE/CHORUS
The thickness of air

WHITE DOVE
Riding the ions

Billowing cloudbanks
Silvery veil on the mountains

WHITE DOVE/CHORUS
The rustling of the air

WHITE DOVE
Shadows on the sky
Ice clouds on the horizon
Flying lines of force

WHITE DOVE/CHORUS
The thicker air below

WHITE DOVE
Mountains glowing red
Clouds like lumps of gold

WHITE DOVE/CHORUS
Whistling of the air
Incandescent clouds
Roaring in the air
The blinding light
The blinding light (repeats)

MUSIC continues. LIGHT gradually stronger, becoming unbearably bright, ALL react to it. End SCENE 4.

Projection image from Violet Fire, *Scene 4: composite image including historic illustration of light bulb, flock of pigeons*

Score for Violet Fire by Jon Gibson, p. 99, Scene 5, "Light the flame within our hearts," Courtesy Estate of Jon Gibson

SCENE 5

PARK. TESLA sits on bench, surrounded by PIGEONS. WHITE DOVE is among them. Projection: CITY LIGHTS/STARS and related images.

REPORTER enters.

> REPORTER
> At night and in secret,
> Nikola Tesla lavishes
> His love on pigeons.
> He calls them down
> From where he stands
> Scatters the seed on the grass
>
> The Great Inventor's getting older
> Hasn't had an investor
> In more than twenty years.
> No one would believe
> The lights around here
> All run on his system.
> What's he dreaming still?

What does it look like
From behind his eyes?

TESLA

People are heartless,
They are inhuman
My dear ones must be fed
My dear ones must be fed

REPORTER

Each year on his birthday
Reporters know the old inventor
Will have a startling story:
"Power by Radio Predicted For Near Future."

Background: images changing to reflect developments in scene:
a WEB FILLING IN, STORM-LIKE PHENOMENA, PULSING
LIGHT, PERIOD VISIONS OF FUTURE, etc.

TESLA

The world was not prepared
I was too far ahead of time

The laws of Nature will prevail
My World System will return
Radio waves disturbing the air

WHITE DOVE

The thickness of air
Flying through moonlight

TESLA

Great standing waves
Disturbing the earth

WHITE DOVE

Silvery veil on the mountain
Do not disturb

REPORTER

"Tesla to Turn Earth
Into One Gigantic Dynamo"

TESLA

The earth is responsive to certain vibrations
Set it ringing, excite the globe
Energy everywhere, free for all

WHITE DOVE

Earth is responsive
Do not disturb

KATHARINE JOHNSON enters, slowly approaches
TESLA through the following.

REPORTER

"Tesla Predicts More Wonders —
Annihilation of Distance
Transmission of Intelligence and Energy
And even Transport of Materials."

Performance photo from Violet Fire,
Scene 5: White Dove (singer, Mirjana Jovanović
Stojanović), with atmospheric conductance
diagram in projection. Photo by Srdjan Mihič

Performance photo from Violet Fire, *Scene 5: l-r, Katharine Johnson (Dragana Stanković), Tesla (Scott Murphree), Chorus members in background. Photo by Srdjan Mihič*

TESLA

The network all done
The web filling in
Bees in the hive
All working as one
Mind touching mind
Energy free for all
An end to suffering

KATHARINE

Something's not right
It's all gone too far
Prometheus, you brought us fire
But your fire isn't right
Burns into the skin
Bores into the brain
All your great invention
All your grand intentions
Will ruin us
We should not have listened
It's all gone too far (repeats)
My head hurts!
My head hurts! (repeats)

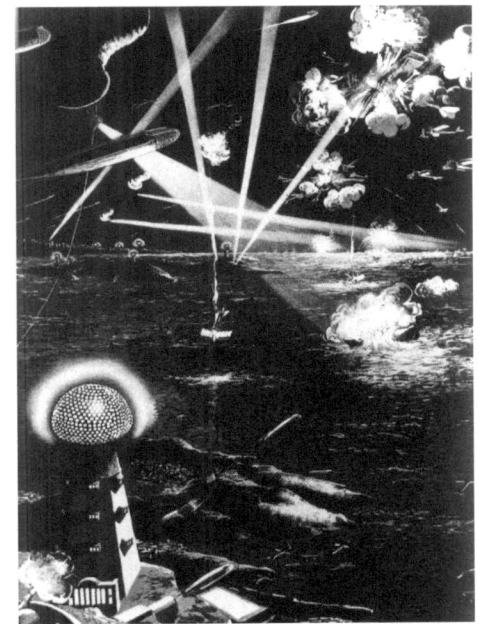

TESLA

I brought a better life
Why don't they understand
Amazing Stories yet to tell
They are so slow to see

WHITE DOVE

Cracks in the earth
Cracks in the air
Beating of wings
Beating of heart
Beating of earth
Earth out of tune

REPORTER

"Tesla to Reveal New Invention
Death Ray for Defense
Inventor Gives World Death Beam
To End War Forever"

TESLA

The time is right, a simple matter
Peace for all—an end to suffering

Projection image from Violet Fire, *Scene 5: composite image of Tesla's Wardenclyffe Tower in negative against image of video static*

WHITE DOVE
Beating of wings

KATHARINE
Something not right

WHITE DOVE
Cracks in the air

WHITE DOVE crouches and folds inward.

KATHARINE
A fire too strange for
Creatures of the earth,
Creatures of the air
Your dreams have made us
Birds in the mine
Creeping disease
Death and destruction
Murderer!
Murderer!

Projection image from Violet Fire, *Scene 5: composite image of White Dove (dancer, Joanna Kotze), pigeon wings, Wardenclyffe Tower*

Performance photo from Violet Fire, *Scene 5, White Dove (Joanna Kotze) dying. Photo by Srdjan Mihič*

TESLA

No! A gift, an end to suffering,

An end —

WHITE DOVE dies. In projection, her outline glows and grows into huge pulsating AURA, encompassing many images. MUSIC. TESLA turns his back to audience, watching this.

PROJECTIONS slowly fade.

REPORTER

"Tesla Sure Life Exists

On Other Planets

Has Plan to Signal Mars

Hello Mars!"

MARGARET STORM enters.

STORM

Prince of the Violet Fire

Native of Venus!

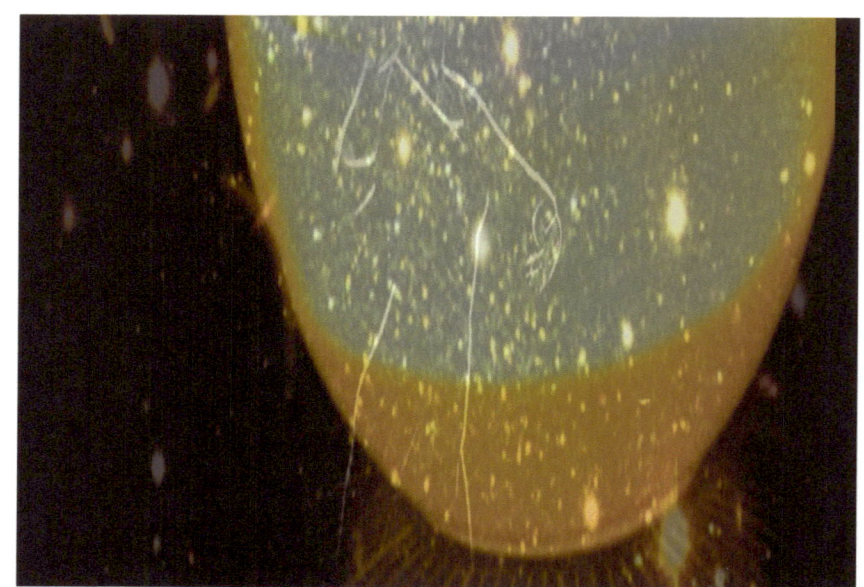

Projection image from Violet Fire,
Scene 4: composite video of
silhouette of Margaret Storm,
planetary model, and field of
stars/galaxies

REPORTER
"Interplanetary Radio
Distance Means Nothing
Tesla Will Use Earth's
Electrical Envelope
To Send Power Out to Planets."

STORM with CHORUS
Prince of the Violet Fire
Emissary from the second planet
Transmute our discordant energies
Raise our finer fibers
Send the cleansing fire

TESLA
I will send power

STORM with CHORUS
The radiant flame
You, adept on higher planes
Visitor from starry space

Hello Mars!

By H. WINFIELD SECOR

Sending of Messages to Planets Predicted by Dr. Tesla on Birthday

Inventor, 81, Talks of Key to Interstellar Transmission and Tube to Produce Radium Copiously and Cheaply— Decorated by Yugoslavia and Czechoslovakia

---

With angelic entities
In the bodies of doves

TESLA
An end to suffering, an end

KATHARINE
No one is listening
Look what you've done

STORM with CHORUS
Come to us on healing wings of peace
Light the flame within our hearts
Light the flame within our hearts

MUSIC/LIGHTNING UP. Meteor showers, planetary bodies.
End SCENE 5.

Above: "Hello Mars!" Headline, article in the Electrical Experimenter *by H. Winfield Secor, April 1920*

Below: "Sending of Messages to Planets Predicted by Tesla on Birthday," Headline, New York Times, *July 11, 1937*

Score for Violet Fire by Jon Gibson, p. 121, Scene 5-6, "Come fly into the cloud-bank," Courtesy Estate of Jon Gibson

SCENE 6

TESLA'S ROOM. TESLA standing as before. Coils spark on during the following. Projections: AURA of last scene slowly returns. KATHARINE, WHITE DOVE, MARGARET STORM surround TESLA in a protective tableau.

                              TESLA
          I was just a boy. The hills rose gray
          Behind the farm. Snow on my hair
          Fingers so cold. My boots made pools
          Of purple light in the darkness.
          I came into the house
          Bent to stroke the cat
          —A miracle! His back
          A sheet of light around my hand.
          A shower of cutting sparks
          A halo like the saints
          Father called it
          Electricity.
          Is nature a giant cat?
          If so, who strokes its back?
          I thought, it must be God.

He stands, and the tableau of WOMEN separates.

Performance photo from Violet Fire, Scene 6. Above, Tesla (Scott Murphree) with White Dove (singer, Mirjana Jovanović Stojanović); below, front, l-r: Reporter (Nenad Nenić), Margaret Storm (Ana Lackovich), Mark Twain (Miodrag Jovanović), Chorus in background. Photo by Srdjan Mihič

TESLA

And when I close my eyes
The lightning is still there
Tongues of living flame
Sheets of pulsing light
Shower of cutting sparks
Haloes like the saints
One hundred million volts
Burning my eyes

WHITE DOVE

Your wish is not granted
The end is not what you think
Give them time to take it in
Come fly into the cloudbank

WHITE DOVE & CHORUS

The mist lies heavy
On the mountains
Let the web fill in
Your wish is granted

TESLA

The fire still burns
Sheets of pulsing light

Coils SPARK UP brighter and louder.

ALL (except TESLA)

Fly into the cloudbank
Sink into the dreambank
Take comfort in the dark
One hundred million volts
Fly into the dark
Sink into the dream
Lay down the fire
Lay down the fire
Now we are all mourning doves
(repeat from "Fly into the cloudbank...")

WHITE DOVE separates from others, standing higher. She reaches
for TESLA, he goes to her. They ascend.

END

Below: Projection image from Violet Fire, Scene 5: composite image of Nikola Tesla, aged 77 (portrait by Sarony, 1933), against skyline of New York and planetary bodies

APPENDICES

Previous page: Portrait of Nikola Tesla, aged 77, by Sarony, 1933

NIKOLA TESLA: A Biographical Timeline

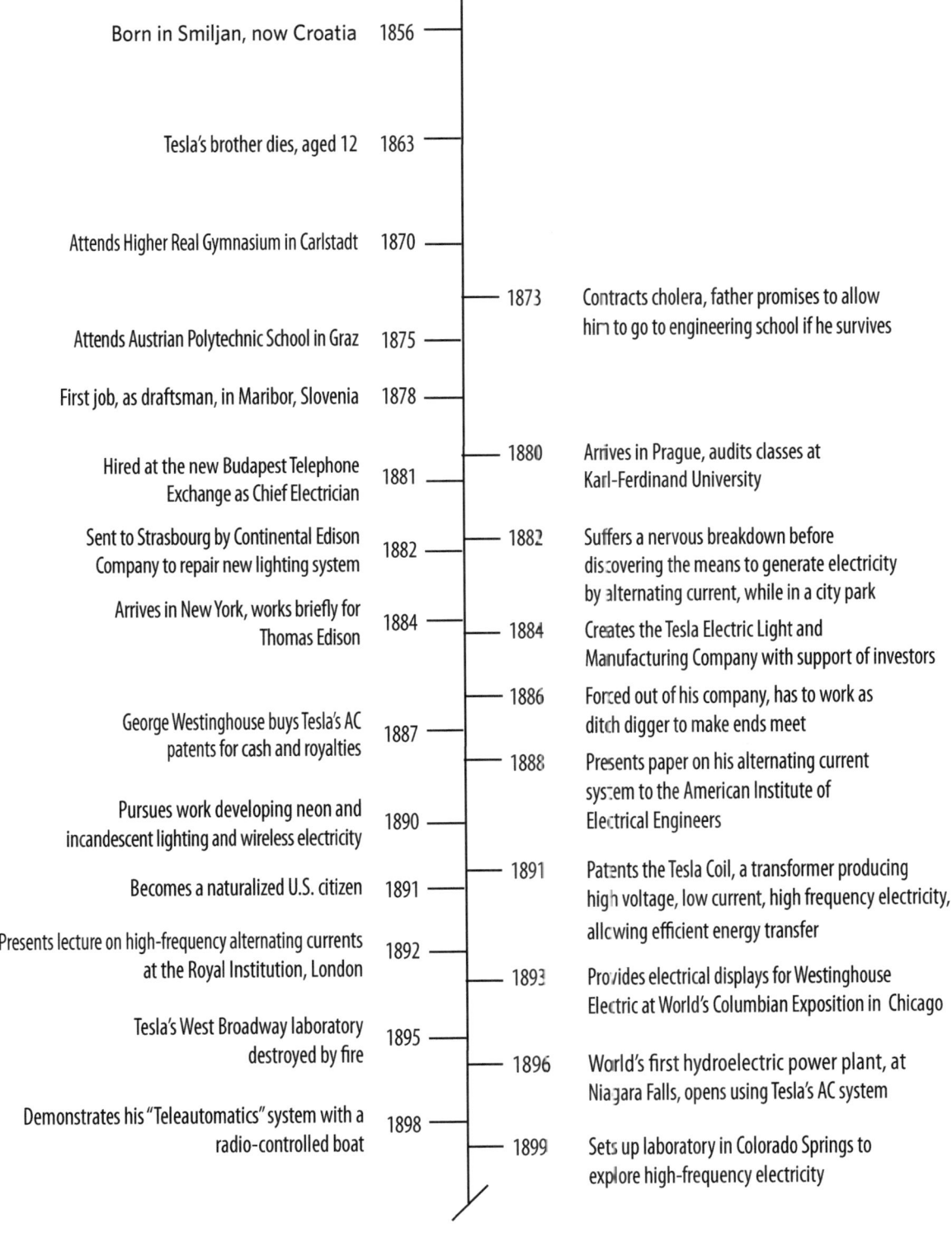

Born in Smiljan, now Croatia — **1856**

Tesla's brother dies, aged 12 — **1863**

Attends Higher Real Gymnasium in Carlstadt — **1870**

1873 — Contracts cholera, father promises to allow him to go to engineering school if he survives

Attends Austrian Polytechnic School in Graz — **1875**

First job, as draftsman, in Maribor, Slovenia — **1878**

1880 — Arrives in Prague, audits classes at Karl-Ferdinand University

Hired at the new Budapest Telephone Exchange as Chief Electrician — **1881**

Sent to Strasbourg by Continental Edison Company to repair new lighting system — **1882**

1882 — Suffers a nervous breakdown before discovering the means to generate electricity by alternating current, while in a city park

Arrives in New York, works briefly for Thomas Edison — **1884**

1884 — Creates the Tesla Electric Light and Manufacturing Company with support of investors

1886 — Forced out of his company, has to work as ditch digger to make ends meet

George Westinghouse buys Tesla's AC patents for cash and royalties — **1887**

1888 — Presents paper on his alternating current system to the American Institute of Electrical Engineers

Pursues work developing neon and incandescent lighting and wireless electricity — **1890**

Becomes a naturalized U.S. citizen — **1891**

1891 — Patents the Tesla Coil, a transformer producing high voltage, low current, high frequency electricity, allowing efficient energy transfer

Presents lecture on high-frequency alternating currents at the Royal Institution, London — **1892**

1893 — Provides electrical displays for Westinghouse Electric at World's Columbian Exposition in Chicago

Tesla's West Broadway laboratory destroyed by fire — **1895**

1896 — World's first hydroelectric power plant, at Niagara Falls, opens using Tesla's AC system

Demonstrates his "Teleautomatics" system with a radio-controlled boat — **1898**

1899 — Sets up laboratory in Colorado Springs to explore high-frequency electricity

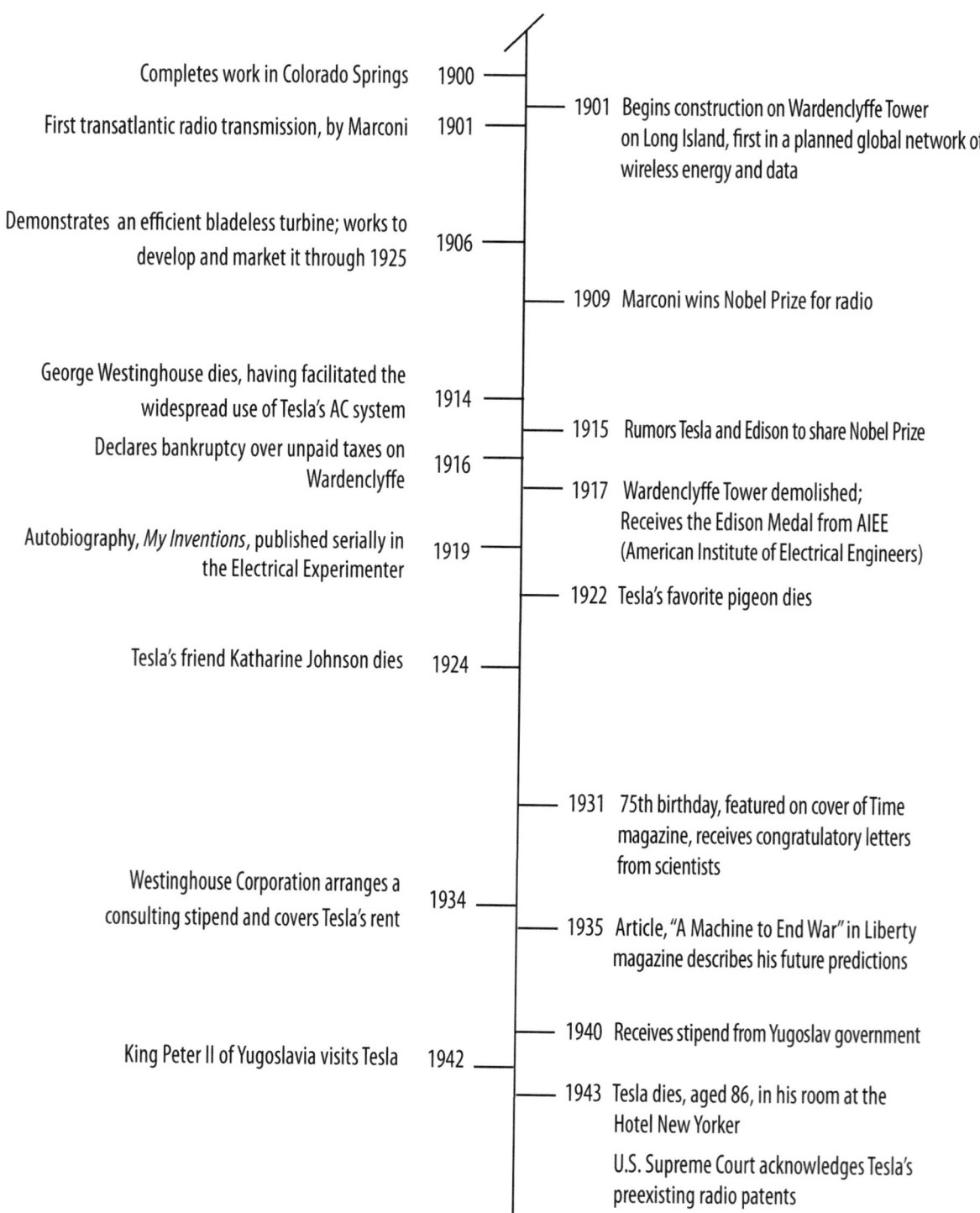

Completes work in Colorado Springs — **1900**

First transatlantic radio transmission, by Marconi — **1901**

1901 — Begins construction on Wardenclyffe Tower on Long Island, first in a planned global network of wireless energy and data

Demonstrates an efficient bladeless turbine; works to develop and market it through 1925 — **1906**

1909 — Marconi wins Nobel Prize for radio

George Westinghouse dies, having facilitated the widespread use of Tesla's AC system — **1914**

1915 — Rumors Tesla and Edison to share Nobel Prize

Declares bankruptcy over unpaid taxes on Wardenclyffe — **1916**

1917 — Wardenclyffe Tower demolished; Receives the Edison Medal from AIEE (American Institute of Electrical Engineers)

Autobiography, *My Inventions*, published serially in the Electrical Experimenter — **1919**

1922 — Tesla's favorite pigeon dies

Tesla's friend Katharine Johnson dies — **1924**

1931 — 75th birthday, featured on cover of Time magazine, receives congratulatory letters from scientists

Westinghouse Corporation arranges a consulting stipend and covers Tesla's rent — **1934**

1935 — Article, "A Machine to End War" in Liberty magazine describes his future predictions

1940 — Receives stipend from Yugoslav government

King Peter II of Yugoslavia visits Tesla — **1942**

1943 — Tesla dies, aged 86, in his room at the Hotel New Yorker

U.S. Supreme Court acknowledges Tesla's preexisting radio patents

TESLA AND GERNSBACK:
An Untold Influence on the Birth of Modern Science Fiction

The relationship between Hugo Gernsback and Nikola Tesla is hidden in plain sight in the pages of Gernsback's early publications. Yet the influence of the older inventor on the younger publisher and writer has never been closely examined, and it can shed new light on the emergence of modern science fiction. To put it conservatively, I believe that Nikola Tesla and his inventions and ideas had a profound influence on Hugo Gernsback during the period that Gernsback felt was formative to his understanding of science fiction—the twenty years or so before he launched *Amazing Stories*.

Hugo Gernsback (1884–1967), a writer, publisher, and sometime inventor, is credited with a generative role in the birth of the science fiction genre as the publisher of *Amazing Stories*, the first English-language magazine devoted to science fiction. Nikola Tesla (1856–1943) is credited with pioneering a number of new scientific fields through his breakthroughs in alternating current, radio, robotics, and even computer circuitry.

Both men were born in Europe—Gernsback to a prosperous Jewish family in Luxembourg and Tesla to a Serbian family of clerics in Croatia—and then emigrated to the United States, and both settled in New York. Both had received fine European educations: Tesla studied at the Realschule in Karlstadt, the Polytechnic Institute in Graz, Austria; and the University of Prague. Gernsback studied at the University in Bingen in Germany.

Above Left: Portrait of Nikola Tesla, age 34, by Napoleon Sarony, 1894.

Above Right: Portrait of Hugo Gernsback by Bachrach, date unknown, reproduced in Radio-Electronics *magazine, November 1967*

Gernsback idolized Tesla. He said he had heard of Tesla as a young teenager in Luxembourg during the first flush of Tesla's fame in the 1890s. Tesla had come to New York after his discovery in 1882 of the rotating magnetic field, a breakthrough that made the development of alternating current possible. By the 1890s, he had gained international fame for this as well as for his experiments in wireless transmission. News of his work spread through the mainstream and scientific press and lectures in the US and England.

Meanwhile the teenaged Gernsback was inspired to offer his services to neighbors setting up electric doorbell systems for them. The Carmelite church in Brussels memorialized his achievement with a certificate of appreciation, dated 1898, dubbing the thirteen-year-old Hugo Gernsbacher an "aspiring electrician." Gernsback later wrote of this formative time, "While studying abroad I read every scrap of [Tesla's] work I could lay my hands on. I performed most of his high-frequency experiments, and the more I saw of his work the more imprest [sic] I became." While in university, Gernsback invented an innovative, high-amperage dry-cell battery. It was with the hope of developing it for commercial use that he emigrated to the U.S. in 1904 at the age of 19. (His dreams of life in America had been nourished by the Westerns he had read as a youth; he signed the first article he published in the US as "Huck Gernsbacher.")

After patenting his battery, Gernsback sold it to the Packard Motor Company and used the proceeds to start up the Electro Importing Company in New York. The company sold electrical components imported from Germany, but most notably gave Gernsback a springboard into publishing. What began as the company catalogue in 1908 quickly morphed into his first journal, *Modern Electrics*. It carried both technical articles and examples of what Gernsback called "scientifiction," including his own twelve-part serial, later published as the novel *Ralph 124C 41+*.

Gernsback was in his twenties and editing *Modern Electrics* when he first met Tesla. Though he had revered Tesla already, Gernsback was still impressed. He later wrote, "I was fascinated with the tall, gaunt man, then about 50 years old. His extraordinary face, with his deep set blue eyes, proclaimed the intense thinker—the philosopher." Gernsback offered his own, somewhat hyperbolic declaration of Tesla's greatness in an article in a 1919 issue of the *Electrical Experimenter*:

> If you mean the man who really invented, in other words, originated and discovered—not merely improved what had already been invented by others, then without a shade of doubt, Nikola Tesla is the world's greatest inventor, not only at present, but in all history.... His basic as well as revolutionary discoveries, for sheer audacity, have no equal in the annals of the intellectual world.

The article offered a cogent summary of Tesla's achievements and their significance, and some reasons why, even then, Tesla wasn't as widely known as Gernsback believed he should be.

The two men met several times over the next few years. By this time, much of Tesla's major work was behind him. He had overseen the creation of the first large-scale hydroelectric power plant, at Niagara Falls in 1896. In 1898, he had demonstrated the first-ever remote-controlled vehicle, a 4-foot-long, steel-hulled boat. He had completed a year of experimentation on high frequencies in Colorado Springs in 1899, where he built a magnifying transmitter, producing extremely high voltages. He had also begun work on his World Broadcasting System.

Tesla's research in Colorado Springs served as groundwork for his planned World Broadcasting System. This project was to be the culmination of Tesla's life work: a massively ambitious plan to transmit not only signals but also electrical energy across long distances with a global network of transmission towers. With the backing of J. P. Morgan, he was able to begin construction of the first tower, called Wardenclyffe, on Long Island's North Shore. It's not too much of a stretch to view it as a planned global communications network predating the Internet. But Morgan withdrew his support, and the tower never went online. The project began in 1901, and the tower was demolished in 1917. Tesla was devastated, not only personally but also financially, by Wardenclyffe's failure.

After the destruction of Wardenclyffe, Tesla continued to work, but he became known more as what we'd now call a futurist. Reporters sought him out for dramatic predictions, some of which featured potential applications of his ideas. In his last years, he was kept from dire poverty by a pension given to him by the Yugoslav government. He died in 1943.

Tesla posing near high-frequency Tesla coils in his Colorado Springs laboratory, 1899-1900

At every point in his career, Tesla showed himself to be a master of self-promotion. He wooed members of the press and celebrities including Mark Twain, inviting them to his laboratory for staged demonstrations. Tesla needed strong financial backing in order to pursue his often extravagantly large-scale projects. A famous photograph of Tesla in Colorado Springs, sitting calmly reading a book next to his magnifying transmitter as it emits cascades of lightning-like currents, was actually a double exposure, staged for maximum effect. So when Gernsback met with Tesla and proposed articles covering his work, Tesla undoubtedly appreciated the appearance of an enthusiastic young man representing a new media outlet. Earlier in his career, in the 1880s and 1890s, Tesla had often been featured in the pages of the many electrical magazines of the time, including the *Electrical Engineer, American Electrician, Electrical Review,* and *Electrical World*; his announcements were carried in the popular press, and he contributed his own writing to *Century* magazine, edited by his friend Robert Johnson.

Yet their first meeting occurred at a difficult time for Tesla. He had been forced to mortgage the Wardenclyffe property to pay its back rent, and the project's future looked bleak. In 1916 he would be forced to declare bankruptcy. Tesla, always open to further publicity, must have hoped that Gernsback's interest might help turn around his business fortunes. And Gernsback, although late to the party in terms of celebrating Tesla's achievements, was happy to oblige. He ran an interview with Tesla in the *Electrical Experimenter*, which he'd begun in 1915. This was followed by an editorial about Edison and Tesla, instigated by the premature and incorrect news that they were going to share the Nobel Prize.

In the editorial, Gernsback makes clear his opinion of the relative scope of Edison's and Tesla's achievements:

> Without wishing to minimize Edison's tremendous amount of work, the fact is well known that he is not so much an original inventor as a genius in perfecting existing inventions.... In this respect Tesla has perhaps been the reverse, for he has to his credit a number of brilliant as well as original inventions....

From this point on, Gernsback's epic devotion to Tesla is closely documented in the pages of the *Electrical Experimenter*. Hugo had begun as an aspiring inventor. He was knowledgeable enough to understand the scope of Tesla's achievements, and his vivid imagination eagerly fed on Tesla's tendency to extrapolate his ideas into large-scale, even global-scale, potential applications. On Tesla's side, I believe he must have responded warmly to Gernsback's appreciation. And a new avenue for publicizing his work would have been very welcome.

Over the next several years, Tesla contributed five articles to the *Electrical Experimenter*. And the magazine churned out articles on Tesla's inventions, offering a virtual retrospective of his accomplishments till then. They included illustrated pieces on several high-frequency transformers or Tesla coils; on his experiments in Colorado Springs in ultra-high frequency transmission (February 1914); on his work in Teleautomatics, as he called it, or remote-controlled robotics, illustrating the radio-controlled boat he had built and successfully demonstrated in 1898 (June 1916); and on his World Broadcasting System (March 1916).

The collaboration between Tesla and Gernsback reached its peak when Gernsback commissioned Tesla to write his autobiography, which appeared in six installments in the *Electrical Experimenter* in 1919. This was later published in book form with the title *My Inventions*, and it is Tesla's only autobiography.

Gernsback and his writers turned out more articles that explored the fertile ground provided by Tesla for speculation about future technologies. For example, "The Utilization of the Sun's Energy" (March 1916) explored possibilities of solar energy. In another article, Tesla announces that his new wireless transmission system would allow him to send light out over the ocean to make shipping lanes safer ("Tesla Has Wireless to Light the Whole Ocean," April 1915).

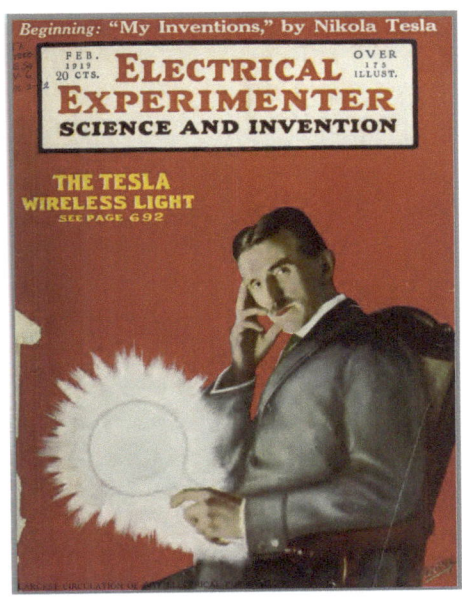

In a later article ("'Cold Fire': Charging the Body with High Frequency Currents," November 1919), Gernsback took a lighter approach. He interviewed Tesla about his experiences using his own (carefully grounded) body to conduct high-frequency circuits from his oscillating coils and reported on undergoing the experience himself. The caption on the fanciful illustration describes the cleansing effects of a "dry bath" with a Tesla coil, and declares, "Every homewill soon be [equipped] with a huge Tesla coil."

With his usual brio, Gernsback didn't hesitate to overinterpret some of Tesla's experimental findings. Gernsback claimed to have been inspired as a child by Percival Lowell's theories about Martian "canals," and remained obsessed along with much of the public by the idea of intelligent life on Mars. While Tesla was in Colorado, he had picked up some signals that he identified as extra-planetary in origin. They were in fact cosmic rays, and he was the first to detect them. Tesla never associated them with inhabitants of Mars. But in the article "Hello Mars! Shall We Ever Be Able to Signal Mars Intelligently?" (April 1920), the author refers to Tesla's work to buttress the plausibility of his speculations.

"The Magnetic Storm," a 1918 story by Gernsback, shows his syncretizing imagination at work. It's presented as reportage, but it's actually an up-to-the-minute science fiction story involving secret technology used against the Germans during the last year of the Great War; a spunky young inventor named "Why" Sparks; and Nikola Tesla himself.

Above: Cover image, Electrical Experimenter, *February 1919, with illustration of Tesla holding a wirelessly powered lamp*

The US had entered the war just months before, and armistice would come that November. We can read between the lines in this story to find a strong emotional investment by Gernsback, who was culturally German, in finding a way to prove his patriotism toward the US and at the same time to "Beat the Huns."

Sparks, the young inventor in the story, is a transparently wish-fulfilling fantasy for the kid inventor Gernsback once saw himself as becoming. In the story, young Sparks comes up with a way to send a kind of huge electromagnetic pulse—a strikingly Teslian idea—behind enemy lines, which will disable all German electric devices and communications networks. Tesla, a benign mentor figure here, congratulates the young inventor for his brilliant idea. The accompanying illustration seems to bear a deliberate resemblance to Tesla's Colorado Springs laboratory.

This story entangles Tesla and his ideas in such a striking way with Gernsback's own imagination and with his impulse to create "scientificion" stories, that it can be seen as offering a kind of Rosetta Stone, a blinking-neon key to the origins of Gernsback's vision of science fiction.

In 1920, *The Electrical Experimenter*'s name changed to *Science and Invention*. It continued to run articles on scientific advances and their potential, on radio construction, contests for inventions, and serialized science fiction by various authors until 1931. It wasn't till 1926 that Gernsback began publishing *Amazing Stories*, now acknowledged as the first science fiction magazine. Gary Westfahl, who has written several books about Gernsback and his legacy, dates the beginning of the science fiction genre to the debut of *Amazing Stories* in 1926.

The authors featured in that first issue—including H. G. Wells, Jules Verne, and Edgar Allan Poe, signaled that Gernsback was very aware of the literary precedents he wanted to build on. Wells and Verne, at least, fell in line with Gernsback's vision of the new genre as one where a story is built around a selected scientific principle as opposed to the fantastic adventure fiction already appearing in other fiction magazines.

Above: Illustration for short story, "The Magnetic Storm," by Hugo Gernsback, Electrical Experimenter, *August 1918. Reprinted in* Amazing Stories, *vol. 1 no. 4, 1926*

Although Gernsback himself had written science fiction, none of it appeared in the pages of *Amazing Stories*. In fact, he doesn't seem to have written any fiction after 1918. His two novels, *Ralph 124C 41+ (1925)* and *Baron Münchhausen's Scientific Adventures* (1928) had both originally been published in serial form in his magazines. The first installment of *Ralph 124C 41+* came out in *Modern Electrics* in 1911. Its story takes place in the Swiss Alps and in space. It incorporates an impressive number of predictions of future technology including Helio-Dynamophores (solar panels), picture phones, and centrally charged electric cars. The hero, whose last name is a punnish wordplay for "one to foresee for one another," saves his love interest by averting an avalanche using a remote beam of energy—again, a very Teslian conceit.

By the time Gernsback debuted *Amazing Stories*, he seems to have set aside the ambition to be a writer in the new genre he envisioned, for the role of identifying, shepherding, and promoting the writing of others. And what of Tesla's role in offering a template for imagining the future? Gernsback never made that connection explicit. But his devotion to Tesla and his legacy lasted till the end of his life, and he memorialized it in a strikingly concrete way. In 1943, Gernsback received word that Tesla, aged 86, was close to death. He arranged to have a death mask of the inventor made and a sculptural bust produced in electroplated copper from the plaster mask. He then commissioned an artist to create a pyramidal base with Tesla's greatest accomplishments depicted on each facet.

This miniature monument to Tesla sat in Gernsback's office until his own death in 1967—an exemplar of futurism and a silent companion for his private musings. In 1963, the noted photographer Alfred Eisenstaedt conducted a photo shoot of Gernsback for Life magazine. One of the photographs acts as a symbolic double portrait of the two men. It shows Gernsback standing next to the bust of Tesla, leaning in familiarly, caught in what appears to be a casual remark to the inventor. However staged it may have been, the moment encapsulates the intimacy and intensity of Gernsback's feelings toward Tesla.

Above: Cover image, Amazing Stories, August 1927

Tesla's ideas and inventions—their global and sometimes cosmic scale and their engagement with higher (invisible) frequencies and frictionless transfer—inspired others in addition to Gernsback. As early as 1901, several years before the two men met, an adventure serial appeared in the boy's magazine *Golden Hours*. "To Mars with Tesla," by Weldon B. Cobb, featured Tesla as a character along with his fictional nephew Young Edison as a sidekick.

Since the fictional appearances that emerged during his life, Tesla has continued to evolve into a kind of science-wizard persona in popular culture through a continuing stream of books, movies, games, and music. Tesla or his more or less mythologized persona has become a touchstone of steampunk in novels such as Scott Westerfeld's *Goliath*, in literary novels including Samantha Hunt's *The Invention of Everything* and Andrei Codrescu's *Messi@h*, and in numerous graphic novels. In film and TV, Tesla has appeared in the movie *The Prestige* (based on the novel by Christopher Priest) and *The Current War*. Numerous books, games, and films use a "secret invention" by Tesla as the MacGuffin to power their plots.

Tesla's inspirational role for Gernsback spanned many years and was grounded in a long-lasting personal relationship. It went beyond the puppy love of Gernsback's early years and his young inventor's fantasy of being mentored by Tesla (as evidenced by "Why" Sparks). Gernsback remained open to Tesla's remarkable turn of mind, which always extrapolated ideas out to the greatest scale of possibilities—not simply producing inventions but projecting the implications of his inventions into the future, especially when they manifestly didn't fit into the present. Even Tesla's projects that were realized—the worldwide electric grid, controlling machines at a distance—have a speculative fiction feel once we rub off the patina of familiarity. And that's without considering some of his other, unrealized ideas like splitting the earth by using magnifying resonant frequencies or drawing electricity down from the ionosphere. This grand-scale way of imagining things resonated with Gernsback's own way of thinking so strongly that we can fairly describe Tesla as a muse for Gernsback.

On Gernsback's side, we have a man who was a minor inventor, a minor writer, and a gifted promoter, a man who had a gift for thinking big, who was inspired by scientific progress and possibilities and who saw the potential of science fiction as an arena for the public imagination. In a noted "double portrait" by Eisenstaedt of Gernsback with Tesla's death mask, we see two kindred spirits, connected beyond the grave, who shared a paradigm-shifting orientation toward the future and shared in the project of creating a literary genre oriented toward the future as well.

—Mir Seidel

This article originally appeared in the New York Review of Science Fiction, *June 2021.*

Violet Fire Collaborators and Performers

Jon Gibson (Composer, 1940-2020) was a pioneering figure in the minimalist movement as a multi-instrumentalist, collaborator and composer. He was a founding member of the Philip Glass Ensemble, and took part in numerous landmark musical events, performing in the early works of Glass, Steve Reich, and Terry Riley among others. He created a large body of works from the late 1960s on—solo and ensemble, instrumental and vocal—which have been performed throughout the world. Gibson collaborated with Nancy Topf, Thomas Buckner, Nina Winthrop, Elisabetta Vittoni, Lucinda Childs, the Merce Cunningham Dance Company, Jaron Lanier, and with director JoAnne Akalaitis on *Voyage of the Beagle*, a music theater work centered around Charles Darwin. His music can be heard on the Orange Mountain Music, New Tone, Point Music, Lovely Music, EarRational Records and Einstein Records labels.

Miriam Seidel (Concept and libretto) also wrote the libretto for *Judgment of Midas*, an opera with score by composer Kamran Ince, which had its concert premiere in Milwaukee in a co-production with Present Music and Milwaukee Opera Theatre, developed with help from American Opera Projects. Her radio play *Interference*, with sound by composer John J. H. Phillips, was broadcast on New American Radio. Her novel, *The Speed of Clouds*, was published by New Door Books. Her stories and essays have appeared in *Exquisite Corpse*, the *Asteroid Belt Almanac*, and *Calyx*. She covered visual art and dance for many years at the *Philadelphia Inquirer*, *Art in America*, *Dance*, *ArtNews*, and other journals. As Mir Seidel, she's had work published in science-fiction and fantasy magazines including *Bourbon Penn*, the anthology *Breathe*, and the *New York Review of Science Fiction*.

Terry O'Reilly (Director) is a playwright, performer and director. He is a longtime co-artistic director of Mabou Mines, and co-founder of Movement Research, a center for teaching, performance ,and publication. His international work includes performances and productions in Japan, Indonesia, Thailand, China, Hong Kong, Taiwan, Rio de Janeiro, Singapore, Western Europe, the Czech Republic, Poland, Serbia and Montenegro. He directed and co-wrote with Simon Wong a children's puppet play in Hong Kong and Guangxi based on US/Chinese folk stories. He was a senior Fulbright Fellow in aboriginal ritual and theater in Taiwan; his plays there include *My Sunshine Book*, *Flying House/Home* and *Cee Cee and Dee*. His play *Animal Magnetism* was directed by Lee Breuer for its NYC premiere, and presented in China in a new incarnation which he co-directed with Dodd Loomis.

Nina Winthrop (Choreographer) has directed her own company, Nina Winthrop and Dancers, and has choreographed numerous dance works since 1992. Winthrop is committed to multimedia collaborations, and has worked with musicians/composers John Cale, Steve Sacks, Jon Gibson and Gary Lucas; set designers David Auden and Manuel Lutgenhorst; sculptor Jene Highstein; costume designers Anita Evenepoel and Naoko Nagata; filmmakers Morleigh Steinberg and Maria Antelman; lighting designers Peter West, Nicole Pearce, Jared Klein and Oguri; and writer/director/dramaturge Linsey Bostwick, among others. As a dancer, she performed with Wendy Perron, Susan Rethorst, Yoshiko Chuma, Sally Silvers and Kei Takei. She curated Dance Conversations @ The Flea, a free performance and discussion series at Tribeca's Flea Theater.

Sarah Drury (Projection Design) is a media artist working with video and sound across installation, performance and network platforms. Her work with sensing technologies and media focuses on narrative, play and the emergent subject in diverse contexts. Her work *Mechanics of Place*, designed with Hana Iverson, is an augmented reality platform for user-generated virtual public artworks allowing for participation via smartphones. She conceived and directed the collaborative sensor-based performance work *The Walking Project*, with performers "speaking" the body with dis/abilities. Installations include *The Listening Microphone*, *Voicebox*, *Vocalalia* and *Intervention Chants*. Her work has been presented at venues including ISEA International, Performative Sites, the Brooklyn Museum, the Kitchen, Artists Space, Hallwalls, and the Worldwide Video Festival at The Hague, and has aired on PBS.

Jen Simmons (Projection Design) is a multimedia designer and filmmaker. Her films *Bush for Peace* and *Inclinations* screened at hundreds of festival venues including International Film Festival Rotterdam, Resfest, Festival of New Film and Media: Split, Croatia, Inside Out: Toronto, NewFest: New York, and Free Speech TV. She has designed projection, lighting, scenic and sound for over 300 shows including for Peggy Shaw, Sharon Bridgforth, Lourdes Pérez, Daniel Alexander Jones, Gloria Anzaldúa, Sandra Cisneros, Paul Bonin-Rodriguez, and Cherríe Moraga. From 1992-2000, Jen worked with the Esperanza Center in San Antonio, Texas, a multidisciplinary performance venue for innovative arts and progressive action. She has spoken widely on web standards, particularly HTML and CSS and has been prominent in the deployment of CSS grid layout.

Boris Čakširan (Set and Costume Design) is a choreographer and costume designer based in Belgrade, Serbia. Having worked as a costume designer for over 25 years, he is considered one of Serbia's foremost costume designers for stage, film and television. He is the founder of ERGstatus, an award-winning contemporary dance project. His work as choreographer and director with ERGstatus reflects his belief in the arts as a healing factor in the human community. He has worked in dance education at leading institutions and festivals in Israel, Poland, and Italy. His many international awards include one of the first CEC-ArtsLink fellowships, leading to collaborative performance projects with organizations including GOH Productions, the American-Czechoslovak Marionette Puppet Theatre and the Silesian Dance Theatre of Poland.

Ana Zorana Brajović (Conductor) is Opera Director at the National Theater of Belgrade. Before this she held the post of Assistant Conductor since the age of eighteen. She also gave her first piano recital at the Serbian Academy of Sciences and Arts before she was twenty; was awarded prizes in competitions in Belgrade and Stresa, Italy; and received the annual October Award, the highest award in Belgrade for music achievement. As a Fulbright Scholar, she studied with Gustav Meier at the Peabody Conservatory, during which she performed in a Millennium Stage Concert at the Kennedy Center. For the National Theater Opera House in Belgrade, she has conducted the operas of Mozart, Verdi, Puccini, Rossini, Bizet, Donizetti, Strauss and others.

Belgrade and New York Performance Participants

Violet Fire's Belgrade performance was part of the City of Belgrade's 2006 BELEF summer arts festival, with producing partners the National Theater of Belgrade and the Tesla Museum. The same artistic team and performers staged the US Premiere at the Brooklyn Academy of Music's Next Wave Festival in October 2006. The productions received major support from the Brooklyn Academy of Music, the Trust for Mutual Understanding, the Republic of Serbia's Committee for the Nikola Tesla 150th Anniversary Jubilee, the City of Belgrade Ministry of Culture, the Soros Foundation's Fund for an Open Society—Serbia, and others.

Collaborators

Composer | Jon Gibson
Concept & Libretto | Miriam Seidel
Director | Terry O'Reilly
Assistant Director | Ivana Dragutinović
     Maričić
Conductor | Ana Zorana Brajović
Choreographer | Nina Winthrop
Sets/Costumes | Boris Čakširan
Media Design | Sarah Drury/Jen Simmons
Media Projection | Charlie Hoey
Lighting Design | Mary Louise Geiger
Sound Design | Jorge Cousineau
Producer | Laura Aswad
BELEF Liaison | Aleksandra Delić

Singers and Dancers

Tesla | Scott Murphree/ Darko Dordević
Reporter | Nenad Nenić
Katharine Johnson | Dragana Stanković
White Dove | Mirjana Jovanović Stojanović
White Dove Dancer | Johanna Kotze/
     Kristen Hollinsworth
Margaret Storm | Ana Lackovich
Mark Twain | Peter Stewart (New York)
     Miodrag Jovanović (Belgrade)

Chorus

Natasha Radovanovic
Olivera Krljevic
Ana Nikolic
Jelena Pavlović
Natasha Matic
Zorana Kalapiš
Natasha Drecun
Maja Živković
Ivana Vidmar
Vuk Radonjic

Igor Vujašković
Boris Postovnik
Boris Babik
Alekstandar Tasic
Ivan Kruljac
Danijela Miloševic

Philadelphia Performance Participants

Violet Fire's first production was mounted at Temple University in Philadelphia in 2004. The production involved the collaboration of Temple faculty and students with the core project participants and the Relâche Ensemble. Temple University voice students performed under the supervision of John Douglas, with the Relâche Ensemble playing the instrumental score. This production was supported by the Temple University Provost's Commission on the Arts, the Five-County Arts Fund, the Pennsylvania Council on the Arts, New York State Council on the Arts, Meet the Composer, and individual donors.

Collaborators

John Gibson | Composer
Miriam Seidel | Librettist
Terry O'Reilly | Director
Thaddeus Squire | Music Director
Sarah Drury & Jen Simmons | Media Design
Philip Grosser | Choreography
Dan Boylen & Martin Dallago | Sets
Anthony Hostetter | Lighting Design
Maori Holmes & Heidi Barr | Costumes
Jay Wahl | Assistant Director
Kim Barrosso | Assistant Conductor

Relâche Ensemble

Bob Butryn | sax & clarinet
Andrea Clearfield | keyboard
John Gaarder | bassoon
Michele Kelly | flute
Douglas Mapp | bass
Harvey Price | percussion
Lloyd Shorter | oboe
Aliza Appel | viola

Singers

Kristin Moody | Tesla
Sharon Derstine | Katharine Johnson
Adam Fry | Mark Twain
Julie Snyder | White Dove
Rachel Sutliff | Margaret Storm
Stephanos Tsirakoglou | Reporter

Chorus

Peri Berman
Colin Dill
Emily Good
Michele Jenkins
Denise Ryks

Dancers

Cynthia St. Clair
Jocelyn Isaac
Jennifer Rose

Violet Fire Studio Recording

The studio recording was produced in cooperation with composer Jon Gibson.
Mick Rossi, Producer, Conductor and Music Director
Recording, mix and mastering engineer: Dean Sharenow
Assistant engineers: Ian Kagey, Akihiro Nishimura
Production Assistant: Chen Pratt
Recorded at Vibromonk Studios, Brooklyn, NY, July 2017

Singers

Scott Murphree, tenor | Nikola Tesla
Marie Mascari, soprano | White Dove
Solange Merdinian, contralto |
    Margaret Storm
Katie Geissinger, mezzo soprano |
    Katharine Johnson
Greg Purnhagen, baritone | Reporter
Peter Stewart, bass baritone |
    Mark Twain

Musicians

Mick Rossi | Piano, organ
Antoine Silverman | Violin 1
Rachel Golub | Violin 2
Debra Shufelt | Viola
Wendy Sutter | Cello
Joe Bongiorno | Bass Violin
Andres Sterman | Flute, Piccolo
Matt Dine | Oboe, English Horn
Peter Hess | Clarinet
Frank Cassara | Percussion 1
Charles Descarfino | Percussion 2

Chorus

Philip Anderson
Lisa Bielawa
Joe Chappel
Tomas Crus

Michele Eaton
Bob Osborne
Sadie Rosales
Kirsten Sollek

Resources

VIOLET FIRE

Violet Fire website: https://violetfiretheopera.com

Violet Fire, studio recording of the opera, available from Orange Mountain Music, orangemountainmusic.com/Catalog.htm

NIKOLA TESLA

BOOKS—NONFICTION

Nikola Tesla. *My Inventions*. Tesla's autobiography, first published serially in the *Electrical Experimenter*, 1919. First book edition, Williston, VT: Hart Brothers, with introduction by Ben Johnston, 1982.

John J. O'Neill. *Prodigal Genius: The Life of Nikola Tesla*. New York: Ives Washburn, 1944. The first biography of Tesla, written by the reporter who knew him. Available in various reprints.

Margaret Cheney. *Tesla: Man Out of Time*. Englewood Cliffs, NJ: Prentice Hall, 1981. The classic biography of Tesla.

Marc J. Seifer. *Wizard: The Life and Times of Nikola Tesla: Biography of a Genius*. Secaucus, NJ: Citadel Press, 1998. Excellent, thoroughly researched biography of Tesla.

Jill Jonnes. *Empires of Light: Edison, Tesla, Westinghouse, and the Race to Electrify the World*. New York, NY: Random House, 2004.

W. Bernard Carlson. *Tesla: Inventor of the Electrical Age*. Princeton, NJ: Princeton University Press, 2013. Award-winning historical study of Tesla.

Richard Munson. *Tesla: Inventor of the Modern*. New York, NY: W. W. Norton & Co., 2018.

BOOKS—FICTION

Christopher Priest. *The Prestige*. New York, NY: Tor Books, 1995. A novel about two magicians featuring Tesla.

Andrei Codrescu, *Messi@h*. New York, NY: Simon & Schuster, 1999. A novel of millennial fever in which Tesla plays a role.

Samantha Hunt. *The Invention of Everything Else*. Boston, MA: Houghton Mifflin Harcourt, 2008. Novel concerning the last days of Tesla.

Scott Westerfield, *Goliath*. New York, NY: Simon & Schuster, 2011. Steampunk novel featuring Tesla as a character.

FILMS

The Secret Life of Nikola Tesla, directed by Krsto Papic, Yugoslavian production, 1980

The Prestige, directed by Christopher Nolan, distributed by Buena Vista Pictures, 2006

Tesla, directed by Michael Almereyda, director, distributed by IFC Films, 2000

The Current War, directed by Alfonso Gomez-Rajon, distributed by 101 Studios, 2017

TELEVISION

Robert Uth, Director, *Tesla: Master of Lightning*. PBS, 2000. https://watchdocumentaries.com/tesla-master-of-lightning/

ONLINE

"Tesla Universe," https://teslauniverse.com. Large website with images, timeline, newspaper archive, and more.

Matthew Inman, "Why Nikola Tesla Was the Greatest Geek who Ever Lived" Graphic essay, https://theoatmeal.com/comics/tesla.

"Tesla: Master of Lightning," website created in conjunction with television show, https://www.pbs.org/tesla. Presents a wealth of resources, including teaching guides

Acknowledgments

For the development of this book, my deep thanks go to Marc Estrin and Donna Bister, the forces behind Fomite Press—for believing a book about the opera might be a way to speak to people about Nikola Tesla; and to the contributors, Ana Zorana Brajović, Andrei Codrescu, Merilyn Jackson, and Terry O'Reilly, for offering their unique perspectives on aspects of the opera and on the real, stranger-than-fiction Nikola Tesla. Andrei Codrescu and Merilyn Jackson were aware of the opera from its development in Philadelphia and both wrote about its first production.

Special thanks go to Srdjan Mihič, whose masterful photographs preserved the beautiful interplay of the singers, costumes, sets, and projections on the stage of the National Theater in Belgrade, and to Sarah Drury and Jen Simmons—for creating the stunning visual projections represented here in video stills.

Thanks so much to Nina Winthrop and Mick Rossi, who were extremely helpful in making excerpts from Jon Gibson's score available.

Thanks also to sensitive readers Julia Hough, Phil Kapp, and Lee Weinstein, and to Susan Spangler, Doug Gordon, and Ann deForest for their book design wisdom.

For the development of *Violet Fire*, the opera, my undying gratitude goes to

- Jon Gibson—without his haunting musical score, none of this would have been possible
- Terry O'Reilly—as director, he brought his vision for and deep understanding of the project to guide it from workshop to first performance to world and US premieres
- Nina Winthrop—whose poetic choreography helped bring the White Dove to life
- Media designers Sarah Drury and Jen Simmons for making the dream of a multimedia production a powerful reality
- Ana Zorana Brajović, conductor in Belgrade and New York, and Thaddeus Squire, conductor in Philadelphia, for leading the performances
- Boris Čakširan for costume and set design, ML Geiger for lighting design, and Jorge Cousineau for sound design in Belgrade and New York

For help along the way, thanks go to Hana Iverson and Janice Marks. For the development of the libretto, I'm thankful to the members of the Working Writers Group including Ann de Forest, Doug Gordon, Louis Greenstein, Larry Loebell, David Sanders, and Debra Leigh Scott.

Loving thanks to Steve Seidel for his unending patience, and to my parents, Barbara and Walter Scheiber, for their unwavering enthusiasm and support for the opera.